hire Libraries

THE CORRIDOR
OF CERTAINTY

North Ayrshire Libraries	
007794117	
DON	2.10.15
	£20
W	

THE CORRIDOR
OF CERTAINTY

Geoffrey Boycott

SIMON &
SCHUSTER

London · New York · Sydney · Toronto · New Delhi

A CBS COMPANY

First published in Great Britain by Simon & Schuster UK Ltd, 2014
A CBS COMPANY

Copyright © 2014 by Geoffrey Boycott

This book is copyright under the Berne Convention.
No reproduction without permission.
All rights reserved.

The right of Geoffrey Boycott to be identified as the author
of this work has been asserted by him in accordance with sections
77 and 78 of the Copyright, Designs and Patents Act, 1988.

5 7 9 10 8 6 4

Simon & Schuster UK Ltd
1st Floor
222 Gray's Inn Road
London WC1X 8HB

www.simonandschuster.co.uk

Simon & Schuster Australia, Sydney
Simon & Schuster India, New Delhi

Every reasonable effort has been made to contact
copyright holders of material reproduced in this book. If any
have inadvertently been overlooked, the publishers would be
glad to hear from them and make good in future editions
any errors or omissions brought to their attention.

A CIP catalogue record for this book
is available from the British Library

Hardback ISBN: 978-1-47113-002-1
Ebook ISBN: 978-1-47113-003-8

Typeset in the UK by M Rules
Printed and bound by CPI Group (UK) Ltd, Croydon, CR0 4YY

CONTENTS

INTRODUCTION

Over the years I have written lots of books about cricket but just one autobiography, which was published in 1987. That book was dominated by cricket, because I saw my life purely as a cricketer. Since then I have been asked on numerous occasions to bring my life up to date, however this book is neither just about cricket nor an autobiography – it's a bit of both, covering my recollections of the past, views on the present, righting some wrongs and discussing the issues that are important to me.

For the first time I have 'opened up' about my personal life, something in the past I guarded with the same passion I put into batting, and reflected on how fatherhood altered my priorities.

It has taken more than 11 years for me to be ready to recount the terrifying and painful months spent facing the greatest battle of my life. I was diagnosed with cancer of the tongue on 4 September 2002 and told I would be dead within three months if I did not embark on a gruelling round of treatments. I have been honest about that experience and held nothing back. Even after all this time, it surprised me how emotive and distressing it was to recall the horrific impact those treatments had on my body. It is not what the cancer does to you, but the torture you have to put yourself through to be cured, and the fact that even then, at the back of your mind, you are thinking: 'I might go through all this and still not survive.'

In the darkest moments, I drew on some of my cricketing experiences to help pull me through. I would count off my sessions of radiation with the same determination I counted my runs on the way to scoring another hundred. But unlike cricket, where I reached the top solely down to my own efforts, cancer was not a one-man battle. This time I couldn't have done it on my own. Without the support and bullying encouragement of my wife Rachael, I would not be here now. She has also helped me fill in some of the gaps, parts I had presumably forgotten because I was either too ill at the time to take it in or I had blacked them out as they were too painful to recall.

Rachael and I also wanted to show that dealing with cancer is not just about the person afflicted, it hurts loved ones just as much, as they face the awful task of nursing the sufferer through their treatment, while dealing with their own feelings of fear and despair.

I hope by committing my cancer story to paper it may be of help to anyone who is unlucky enough to be diagnosed with this awful disease. I can understand why some people give up and decide they have had enough, but all I can say is you need a positive outlook and the courage to complete the treatment. That's all you can do; it's what I did, and I am delighted to be here to tell that story.

Such an experience changes your outlook on life and this book is certainly not just about fighting cancer. I've never written before about how I repaired my relationship with Fred

Trueman, and I wanted to try to show the real Brian Clough, two of the greatest characters in British sporting history. Cloughie loved his cricket and was one of my best friends. He was a manager who conquered Europe, not once but twice, with great football and an infectious personality. Sadly, many of the modern generation remember him only as the alcoholic wreck portrayed in the film and book, *The Damned United*.

It is more than 30 years since I last opened the batting for England and my final appearance for Yorkshire was at Scarborough on 12 September 1986. I have never picked up a cricket bat since, not even for charity. I don't want to play if it cannot be at the top. But on that September day, when I walked off the field at 5.21pm, the saddest thing of all for me was that neither the Yorkshire members, the press nor even I knew it was to be my last match. There was no fanfare, no applause, no plaudits.

After playing for the club for 25 years, in 414 matches and scoring 32,570 runs, the ex-players on the Yorkshire cricket committee were so bitter and resentful of my rapport with the members that they deliberately held back their decision it would be my last season. True to form, they gave no thought for anyone else and did not allow my Yorkshire supporters a chance to say goodbye and thank you; nor was there an opportunity for me to thank them. I feel it was a wicked thing to do. In this book I recount my recollections and battles with these committee men, and how I retaliated after some of the old enemies and jealousies resurfaced when I became the club's president in 2012.

But this isn't just a case of me trying to answer my critics. I know I have made mistakes in my life, and growing older has given me a new perspective on events, so I wanted to explore some of those mistakes and assess what I did wrong. I now realise that taking on the captaincy of Yorkshire, and not playing for England for three years, was one of my greatest cricketing regrets.

Listening to Tony Greig's widow at his memorial service prompted me to reflect on one of the great myths of cricket: the Packer series, which so many believe changed the face of the game. I was at the heart of it, and one of only a few left who really knows what went on, so I wanted to set the record straight on this subject that continues to cause debate even now.

Cricket is all I have known for more than 50 years and I have been fortunate to have made two very successful careers out of it. My commentary job takes me all over the world and I have seen at first hand the problems the game faces. The greatest by far is the horrible, modern scourge of sledging, which is dragging cricket down, and our administrators are too weak to do anything about it. I would have no problem dealing with the sledgers!

Of more immediate concern is the state of this England team. Why did Kevin Pietersen's career have to end? How did Australia win the Ashes 5–0 and just what can England do to win back the urn?

These are some of the issues from the past, present and future that interest me, and I hope this book captures them all, for one thing that has never changed is my love for the game of cricket.

Geoffrey Boycott
Boston Spa, Yorkshire
May 2014

CHAPTER I

TROUBLE AND STRIFE

Throughout my cricketing life I have made enemies and I accept it has often been caused by my forthright character, which has sometimes rubbed people up the wrong way. For that I am sorry.

My mother used to say I had tunnel vision. I can hear her now: 'Our Geoff has got blinkers on; he just sees what he wants and goes for it.' She knew from personal experience what I could be like. I once passed Mum in the street near our house and did not even speak to her because I was so deep in thought about my knock earlier that day. She was mortified and in tears when I got home, but I was just thinking about my batting and unable to see the world around me.

I agree that my single-minded approach was a failing in life, but if I upset people it was never intentional – it was just the unfortunate result of a burning desire to get the best out of myself and achieve as much as possible. I did not find it easy to get to the top: I had to fight hard, make the most of my talent and believe in myself. Throughout my teens and early years, people were always telling me I was not good enough and that I would never make it as a cricketer. So, looking back, I think that made me develop a hard outer shell to keep going and stay focused on my goal. This thick skin helped me cope with rejection and gave me the confidence to ignore the doubters, but perhaps it had its downside as well.

During the 1980s, Yorkshire Television ran a programme on which a personality would have their handwriting, palm and horoscopes read. The experts did not know the identity of the person they were assessing, and I remember how the palmist said I was 'an introvert extrovert'. I was somewhat baffled by this description, but Rachael said it summed me up perfectly. She had seen me in new situations appearing to be full of bravado, when she knew that really I was so unsure of myself.

When it came to cricket, there was much less debate about my personality: I was a perfectionist, always striving and never satisfied from the day I started until I retired. When batting, I would shut out all the noise of the crowd, the chirping from other players and just be in my own world concentrating on the ball. Even now, when I play golf, it is impossible to put me off. I still have the ability to shut out all extraneous noise, so if you clap or shout at the top of my backswing or when I'm putting, it doesn't affect my concentration. It is the result of a life spent completely focused on the end goal.

It was reinforced early in my international career when I met the great tennis player Fred Perry. It was early in 1968 and I was a junior member of England's tour squad to the West

Indies. On a drive from Kingston to Montego Bay in Jamaica, we stopped off at a place called the Runaway Bay Hotel. Fred was in charge of the carts at the golf course, hiring them out to the mostly American guests. I was amazed when he came over to talk to me. I was not the star – Colin Cowdrey, Ken Barrington and Tom Graveney were the senior players – but he wanted to talk to me because he said he enjoyed watching my batting.

I would be lying if I said I can remember verbatim what he said to me all these years later, but the general message remains clear in my mind. He told me I had to be focused on myself if I wanted to reach the top and warned me that it can be a lonely, long journey, however if I wanted to be the best I had to have a selfish mindset. He was right. Look at Nick Faldo, who has been compared to me in terms of his character and single-minded approach to his sport. We both had this all-consuming desire to be number one at what we did. What I've learned now is that it is okay to have that mindset, but it should never be to the detriment of others.

It was because of this that I always knew during my career that I did not want the commitment of marriage and children, thinking it would be impossible to do justice to my cricket along with taking on the role of a husband and father. As a professional cricketer, I needed the freedom to go and travel whenever and wherever my job took me.

I met Rachael Swinglehurst on 6 September 1974 at the Lamb Inn, Rainton, near Ripon. Yorkshire had awarded me a benefit that year, and the landlord of the pub organised an event in my honour. I can still remember what she was wearing when we first met, but did not know at the time that it was to be the start of a 40-year, on-off love affair, and she would become the mother of my only child and eventually my wife.

In those days, international tours lasted much longer than they do nowadays. and Rachael would join me when her job allowed, but after our daughter Emma was born in 1988 she was no longer as free to do that.

Rachael was living with her parents near Whitby when the press somehow found out about Emma's birth and, unbeknown to anyone, got a photograph of the little one, aged about six months and printed it on the front page of the *News of the World*. After that they did some despicable things to try to get Rachael to talk, even threatening to print a story that her brother was the father so it must be a case of incest, which eventually forced her to issue a statement confirming I was Emma's father. They even offered her six-figure sums, which is a lot of money now, never mind then, for a kiss-and-tell story, but she wouldn't do it.

From then on, the press were quite relentless in trying to get any information they could about her and Emma, as all my cricketing career I had fiercely guarded my private life from the papers. Rachael hated being constantly followed, so when Emma was nearly two years old, and her parents moved to Tenerife, she decided to go too, and they lived there for a few years.

However, both Rachael and I thought it important that Emma be schooled in England. So when circumstances brought us back together in 1996, my daughter was nearly eight before I first started to get to know her. However, it was not for another three years until she and Rachael came to live with me permanently at my house in Woolley. Wow, that was an awakening!

Suddenly I had this child in my house, someone who took no prisoners – a mini-me, if you like. All my adult life, for differing reasons, I had been indulged by those close to me without fully appreciating it, but not anymore. Emma wasn't bothered about the fact I was a 'celebrity', held in high esteem by millions of cricket fans around the world. As far as she was concerned, I was just her dad, and she believed that role should take priority over anything else.

I was nearly 60 years old and, for the first time in my life, there was this little mite telling me my duties. Sometimes when she asked me to do something, I would say: 'But what if I don't want to do that?' In her mind, it was simple: 'You have to, you're my father.'

Things changed in so many ways. I would be standing at the toilet in the bathroom and she would walk in. I would tell her: 'I'm having a wee,' but her reply would be: 'So, I need to talk to you.' This was totally new territory for me, and it took some getting used to, but I tell her now I wish I'd had three like her. Emma and Rachael both made me realise there is more to being on the planet than cricket and worrying about yourself.

People think it was getting cancer that changed me, and it did. When you fear time is limited, your priorities do change, but it really started a few years before that. Close friends tell me I had become a lot more mellow once my two 'girls' had become my life.

Their influence changed my perception of others, and Rachael played a large part in healing a rift with Fred Trueman. One of my greatest regrets is that I spent 18 years without him in my life. From 1983 to 2001 I had no direct contact whatsoever with Fred, even though we never actually had a cross word. It pains me now to think about all those wasted years not hearing Fred's anecdotes or being around such a unique personality. He was the 'greatest living Yorkshireman', and proof of his legacy is the fact you only have to begin a story with 'Fred' or 'FST' and people know instantly who you are talking about.

I told Rachael and Emma that I idolised Fred from the age of 11, when I went to Headingley for the first time to watch international cricket and saw his Test debut in 1952. In the second innings, India were reduced to 0 for four and bloody terrified of facing Fred, who picked up three wickets in his first eight balls. He had the most perfect action and even now I still marvel over it: sideways on at delivery, looking through the left arm, with a lovely glide to the crease. He was so poised at delivery, it was a thing of beauty watching him run up and bowl the ball.

I first met him in person at the Yorkshire nets in around 1956. By then I was a teenager playing for Barnsley alongside Michael Parkinson and Dickie Bird, and I was invited to practise with the senior players, which was how they judged young cricketers in those days. We did not have purpose-built nets at the time, and instead we had to use the old tea room, which had poor lighting, an uneven surface and of course we had very little protective gear. Fred bowled quickly at everyone – that was his way.

I only found out many years later, after scoring my 100th hundred in 1977, that Fred was asked to give his verdict on me in the nets. He told the BBC in an interview that Arthur Mitchell, the tough old goat who was head coach, asked him to bowl flat out at this 'young 'un'. Fred said he saw this weedy-looking young kid with glasses and a cap on and said: 'Are you sure?' Mitchell replied: 'Ay get stuck in to the little bugger.' After 20 minutes in the nets, he asked Fred for his verdict.

Fred told him: 'He's got a fucking good defence, not easy to get him out, but doesn't have any shots.'

Mitchell said: 'Ay, but just think how good he'll be when we teach 'im to play a few shots.'

It was a great experience to face Fred at that age, and it also meant I was no longer quite so in awe of him when I played alongside him in the first team. It was lovely being on the same side, because it meant I could take the mickey out of him and not worry about having to face his bowling later. Eventually he got his own back, though. We had pre-season nets in Bradford one year and the pitches were wet through and pretty lively. Fred bowled quickly and kept hitting me on the gloves, when I came out of the nets I had bruised hands and the skin on my fingers was ripped off. He came up to me and said: 'I told you I'd get you, you four-eyed little bugger.' He had a long memory.

Of course one of his famous methods to unsettle opponents would be to go into their dressing room before play and pick his targets. Some enjoyed it and looked forward to it happening, others tried every trick in the book to keep him out. Jack Bannister, who had a long career with Warwickshire, tells a lovely story about how they locked the door of their dressing room to keep Fred out before a game in Bradford in the 1960s.

Fred was on 91 wickets in the middle of July and wanted nine more to be the first bowler in the country to reach 100 wickets. 'The first rattle of the door-knob came at 10.30am, followed by five others in the next 35 minutes, before a seventh was accompanied by a voice saying: "Tea lady here with your tea and biscuits." The door was opened and in she came with FS just behind. He stood there like John Wayne entering a hostile Wild West saloon and then delivered his crushing remark: "Right, you lot. I want nine for a hundred, so you can draw lots for who is the odd one out."'

Priceless! You can see why I missed Fred for so many years.

At the heart of our fallout, and so many others in my life, was Yorkshire cricket. When I was sacked as a player in 1983, it tore the club apart. The members rose up and voted to sack the committee and reinstate me as a player. It has been well documented before, so I do not need to go into it again in detail, apart from to place it in the context of my relationship with Fred.

He was on the cricket committee which recommended they sack me at the end of the season. Yorkshire had just won the Sunday League under Ray Illingworth, who was captain and manager, and I had played in 13 of the 16 matches. The club had awarded me a testimonial in 1984 for 20 years' service, so I thought I was in their plans. I had also performed pretty well in the Championship, so sacking me was always going to be a hard sell to the general committee, which was not made up of ex-players.

The thing people always have to keep in mind about Yorkshire cricket is that we are a members' club. It is one member, one vote, regardless of how rich or poor you are, or how many runs or wickets you have to your name. This was something those past players, who had started all the trouble, had forgotten. When the cricket committee did manage to persuade the general committee round to their way of thinking, all hell broke loose. The members forced a special meeting in

Harrogate on 21 January 1984. There were three resolutions: firstly to give Geoffrey Boycott a contract, secondly a vote of no confidence in the cricket committee and thirdly a vote of no confidence in the general committee. All the motions were passed, and the following day both committees had to stand down and hold new elections.

I am not egotistical about it; they did not lose their jobs only because of me. I was just the last straw and the members had seen enough of autocratic committeemen sacking the club's great players. They had sacked Brian Close, forced out Ray Illingworth and even going back to the 1950s they had sacked Johnny Wardle.

It was time to listen to the people, and Fred was now on thin ice. He'd been the most vocal and high profile in trying to persuade the members to back my sacking. There was no doubt that he was chosen to be their spokesman because of his tremendous record and standing in Yorkshire cricket. But then Fred decided to make his biggest mistake: full of bluff and bluster, he announced he would stand for re-election on an anti-Boycott ticket. He promised that if elected he would vote again for me to be sacked. I think he assumed his name and legendary status would guarantee him votes, but it did not. He lost in his ward to a local man who I had never met, a printer named Peter Fretwell, and it was humiliating.

It was amazing to see such an iconic player rejected, and from then on he held me responsible for this embarrassment. This is what Yorkshire cricket does to people; it can be so emotional and irrational. All of Fred's decisions and choices in this controversy were made by him, not me, but he now saw it as my fault that he had lost his seat on the committee. He was very bitter about the whole thing, and from then on no longer went anywhere near the club. He felt betrayed and angry, but what he failed to understand was that the members voted against him not because of his great deeds for Yorkshire but because they felt he had let them down by ignoring their wishes.

After that whenever he gave an after-dinner speech, it seemed he would take any opportunity to rubbish me and lampoon my character. I suffered in silence for years as Fred bad-mouthed me to anyone who would listen, and all contact between us ceased completely. I never once rubbished him and still fondly remembered this great character and bowler. Fred had fallen out with me, not I with him.

Quite a time after everything had happened, I heard Fred on the radio saying that supporters of mine at the time had sent him hate letters and made abusive phone calls, which had upset his wife greatly. Once again, by association I was getting the blame, but in fact I had known nothing about such things, and it was most definitely not something I would have agreed to. I immediately wrote to his wife, Veronica, to explain this to her and to say how sad and sorry I was it had happened. I never received a reply.

Sometime around 2000, I was not writing for a newspaper and was approached to take over Fred's role at the *Sunday People*. I was told that the paper was going to 'retire' Fred as their cricket correspondent. I asked if he knew about this retirement, and was told 'not yet'. While I would have welcomed the job, I decided to turn it down as I did not want Fred blaming me for losing him his job.

By that stage, I was living with Rachael and Emma, and they

would often hear me telling funny stories about Fred, and how I understood why he was angry with me but thought it was irrational and unfair. Rachael is much better at handling people than me. She has a warm personality and is smart at building bridges, so in 2001 she noticed Fred's 70th birthday was looming and persuaded me to send him a birthday card.

I was reluctant at first, because I did not want this gesture thrown back in my face. I thought: 'What is the point? He will only chuck it in the waste paper basket and ignore it the same way my letter to Veronica had gone unanswered years before.' But Rachael chivvied me along, bought a card and I sat down to write it. Obviously, I do not have a copy, but basically I poured it all out, describing him as the greatest living Yorkshireman, as a fast bowler up there with the best ever and recalling how I had admired him ever since his Test debut. I finished by telling him he was a legend in his lifetime.

No reply was forthcoming, but not long after a friend told me Fred's attitude to me had totally changed. He said Fred had been touched by my gesture and immediately taken any nasty or negative things about me out of his after-dinner speeches. A year and a half later, I was diagnosed with cancer and our friendship was rekindled. After I recovered, he and Veronica came to parties at Woolley on a few occasions. Fred would regale all the guests with his lovely stories and jokes. Rachael and I got invited back to their house once for lunch. I even finally persuaded him to start coming to matches at Headingley again after nearly 20 years away.

But think of all those wasted years, all over a row about Yorkshire cricket. I try not to dwell on those bad times, I now just concentrate on Fred the character and Fred the bowler.

During a Test match at Lord's when there had been a rain delay, Michael Atherton once asked me how good he was. During the break, old black and white footage had been shown of Fred bowling in his pomp. These old grainy images always slow down the action, but what I said to Michael was: 'Listen, how good do you think Waqar Younis was? Fred had the same pace as Waqar at his best, but unlike Waqar he could swing it out and cut it back off the seam. He had an outswinging yorker that was lethal. That gives you some idea of how good FST was.'

When I was invited on the Yorkshire board in 2004, I proposed that we nominated some of our former great players for president and put forward Fred's name, which was seconded by the chairman Colin Graves, but sadly we were outvoted three to two. Robin Smith, the deputy chairman, felt it should go to Bob Appleyard instead, so he was made president for 2005 and 2006.

Fred died in the July of Bob's second year, so sadly by the time the position became vacant again, FST was no longer with us. Happily, I did manage to get the board to name something after Fred. I wanted it to be one of the stands at Headingley, but had to settle for an enclosure behind the bowler's arm. Again the saddest thing is he never got to witness and enjoy that either – why do people have to be dead before they get recognised?

I shake my head when I think of the pain caused by Yorkshire cricket down the years and, unlike my relationship with Fred, one of those rifts will never repair.

When the possibility had been mooted in 2010 that I might be nominated by the board for the presidency, unfortunately the old rivalries and problems of the past resurfaced. Two former players came out of the woodwork to raise strong objections. Richard Hutton led the way, but Bob Appleyard later joined him in a bid to stop my taking up the role. For more than 25 years, these two, along with Bob Platt (a big pal of Fred's), appeared to hate me with a passion, and word would often get back to me of some of the things they had said about me. If ever I was in the same room as them, they seemed to avoid making eye contact, and would stand in a huddle whispering to each other.

Hutton disliked me as soon as I became captain of Yorkshire in 1971, and appeared to resent the fact that I was leading the club, an achievement he failed to match. Richard is bitter and I felt had an obsession with me. I have never trashed his cricket ability, and always picked him in my side when I was captain, because he was a good county cricketer, and I respected and admired his father, Leonard's, performances. Len was one of the all-time great batsmen, the first professional to lead England and an Ashes-winning captain. He was loved by the public, but as can often happen his son struggled to live up to the family name.

Richard could never match his father's abilities as a cricketer, but he could have established his own legacy by becoming captain of Yorkshire, a feat that eluded Len, but his chances ended when I got the job ahead of him. I think he has been frustrated about this missed opportunity ever since; indeed, even when we were playing on the same team, I gathered that he made it clear in the dressing room that he was not sorry to see me get out.

Just before it was announced that I was going to be nominated for the 2012–13 presidency, I was in Australia commentating on the Ashes tour and our chairman, Colin Graves, told me the club had received a letter from Richard explaining why I was most unsuitable to be president. Colin and Robin Smith went to see Hutton to try to placate him and to talk him out of continuing in this vein. They even offered to put him forward for a vice-presidency, which he accepted, but he was still not for turning, and fortunately for me, neither were the board.

His letter, sent in November 2010, started with him explaining how he was a past player and came from a family that had 80 years' association with the club. He went on to say: 'The bestowal of the presidency is a considerable honour; of which I do not think Mr Boycott is worthy. His contractual disputes during his playing days brought the club to its knees more than once and damaged its standing and reputation with a wider public. The legacy still stands. Mr Boycott continues to be a controversial and divisive figure. My experience of him is that he is self-seeking and self-serving. There are too many stains on his character for his being the true uniting force that the club should be seeking in its president.'

He carried on with some drivel about the fact I lived in Jersey, which was bound to affect the time I could give to the job, and my refusing to join the Yorkshire past players' association. He even mentioned my unwillingness to help some guy I had never heard of who was writing a book about past players. Apparently, according to him, this showed how disassociated I was with all at Yorkshire cricket. He finished with a flourish saying there was 'considerable and growing' opposition against my becoming president and he 'feared' that some might go public, plunging the club into a 'new dark age'. He concluded by suggesting he would be pleased to meet up and advise the committee in finding a more suitable candidate.

Wow! The same old pompous, superior attitude remained. I thought it was a load of old rubbish. He was still raking over the past, and I pondered for quite a while if I should just ignore it or not. I'd had years of him sniping about me, but this was in a new league. This was a nasty thing to do. To have sent a letter like this to me would have been one thing, but to send it to my chairman and colleague on the Yorkshire board was out of order.

Rachael was as upset by this as I was and said that I should reply. We knew it was not going to change his attitude, but thought that it was time to stop turning the other cheek and give like for like. So I sent a letter to him in June 2011, itemising my response to everything he had brought up.

I began by saying: 'Your misguided self-importance is unbelievable, the more so as you're not even a member. Where were you for the club after your retirement in 1974 to now?' I pointed out that, unlike him, I had been a paying member since 1973, even while playing for the club and only stopped when, with the members' approval, I had been made an honorary life member in 1993. Given that Richard had moved down south, got a job with his wife's father; despite this, it hadn't worked out and he returned to Yorkshire only a few years previously, I told him it was disingenuous to suggest where I lived had anything to do with how I would carry out the role. Furthermore, he knew nothing of my future plans (we had in fact already decided to move back to Yorkshire and were looking for a house).

As regards the past players' association, I pointed out these get-togethers were supposed to be enjoyable, and that wasn't going to happen for me when he and his cronies did nothing but 'slag me off' and could not even bring themselves to acknowledge me. I described his comments about my past contractual disputes with the club as 'a load of tripe', adding that 'the only people who believe that are ones with ulterior motives, who want it to be so, like you; the disputes were about me, but not of my making. I did not sack myself and did nothing to justify such action.' I told him he was being condescending to the members of the time who rose up in revolt.

I pointed out my name, through my own efforts as a player, member, committee man and board member, had been associated with YCCC for nearly 50 years. During that period, I had latterly not received any expenses for my time and in addition had raised a lot of money speaking at events for them free of charge.

On a more personal level, I said he had been hostile to me for years. 'Your father was loved, respected and admired by many people around the world, but particularly in Yorkshire. So many doors have opened to you and opportunities have been given to you because of your father. You have ridden on his coat tails most of your life. It is his name and his achievements – not yours – that give you entry to so many things. All this negativity is both harmful to me and Yorkshire cricket, but quite frankly it does you the most harm. Isn't it time it stopped?' Needless to say, I did not get a reply and am delighted that Richard Hutton never came near the club during my presidency.

Not long after the Hutton episode, Bob Appleyard wrote to

the chairman opening up a different old wound. Bob and I respected each other for our cricketing achievements, but we clashed in the late 1980s, while both elected committee men, over the future of Yorkshire's cricket academy. It was he who had the original idea of an academy; he developed it and deserves all the plaudits for many of the fine players we have produced since its inception. I believe it is the best finishing school in the country, and there are plenty of players in the England side who have benefited from the skills of our coaching staff. Whenever I speak on this subject, I give Bob credit for establishing an academy in the 1990s. But although we agreed over the principles, there was one issue where we differed: where it should be based.

Bob is a Bradford man and at the time the committee also had quite a few other people from the same area. They wanted the academy to be separate from Headingley and suggested it should be established at Bradford Park Avenue, which had been closed for some time and had become derelict. I think Bob hoped moving the academy there would bring investment to the ground, with the view that Yorkshire would eventually return and play championship matches there once again.

I thought that the cost of such an operation was crazy and I pointed this out at committee level. I did not understand why we would want an academy miles away from the club's home. At Headingley we had all the facilities, but if we set up in Bradford we would have had to buy new equipment and spend thousands upgrading and staffing the premises. Although Bob had managed to persuade some local businessmen to sponsor some of the running costs every year, I felt that could not last and that Yorkshire would still have to make up the shortfall –

it was money we could not afford. Regrettably, I was out-voted by the Bradford contingent.

Ten years later, in 1999, the accountants told us the academy would have to close, as it had cost the club in total around an extra £170,000. The original sponsors, as predicted, had stopped giving any money to the club after about three years. There had been no reinvestment in the site, which was a mess, and the academy building was always being broken in to and stuff pinched. When it was moved back to Headingley, Bob Appleyard blamed me for the decision, despite the fact I was not even on the Yorkshire committee, having been voted off in the early 1990s, so I'd had nothing whatsoever to do with the decision. Somehow, perhaps because of my initial opposition, he thought it was my fault.

This old disagreement reared its head when Yorkshire were relegated in 2011. Colin Graves, our chairman, made some very strong comments in the press about the standard of the team's performances, and this prompted Bob to write to him and blame me, for what he perceived to be the lack of talent being produced by the academy. True, I was on the Yorkshire board by this time as the 'cricket' representative, but I had absolutely no power over the academy or anything else for that matter. Stewart Regan, then chief executive, and Martyn Moxon were in charge of that side of things, and (as I was often told by Robin Smith) I merely held an 'honorary position' so could only advise, if ever asked.

In Bob's letter to Colin, he went on to make objections about my personality and even pointed to my court case in France as a reason why I was not suitable to be president. He described as 'the last straw' my letter to Richard Hutton, in which I accused him of living off the family name, an opinion I stand by today. 'The letter is unworthy of a member of the Yorkshire board, let alone that of a future president,' wrote Bob. 'At a time when YCCC needs all the help it can get, I firmly believe we cannot afford conflicts like this ... it is clear the last thing we need is for an exodus of members over a Boycott issue, as happened before.'

His attitude seemed to mellow somewhat after I was asked to give a speech on behalf of Yorkshire cricket at a birthday party held to honour Keith Howard, a generous benefactor of the county. He had donated a lot of money so that Headingley could start a museum, which had recently been opened. I spoke about the tradition and history of our great club and mentioned the obvious, more famous past players. However, I could not leave out Bob from that list, and went on to expand on how he was a great Yorkshire cricketer but an unlucky player. In his first season for the county he took 200 first-class wickets, but contracted tuberculosis and did not play again for two years. He came back, bowled fantastically well and was picked for Len Hutton's tour to Australia in 1954–55. If TB had not depleted his health and shortened his career, he might have been one of the all-time great bowlers. He bowled fast off-cutters from a high action. People think of Derek Underwood and how great he was on uncovered pitches, but Bob bowled with the same pace from a higher trajectory and was lethal.

Rachael, among others, said it was as good a speech as they had ever heard me make. Just as we were leaving, Robin Smith told Rachael that after my speech Bob had remarked to him: 'I think we have got ourselves a new president.' Thereafter, the letters stopped. During my presidency he would come to international games, hosted by me in the Hawke room, and attended many county games also in my presence. I know he can be a cantankerous old so-and-so, and I am not saying we are now bosom buddies, but he was always polite to Rachael and me.

I'm delighted to say that, in the end, they were both proved wrong and their predictions never materialised. There was no 'new dark age' or exodus of members and I spent two very happy years as president. In my first season, we won promotion back to Division One in the championship, and then competed for the title in our 150th year, eventually finishing as runner up. Rachael and I organised and ran many successful events to mark Yorkshire's anniversary, raising between us well over £100,000. At the end of it all, I was asked by quite a few members and their committee men if I would consider doing a third year, but unfortunately the club rules do not allow someone to hold the post for more than two years.

A lot of wasted energy in my life has been spent on sorting out problems and issues at Yorkshire cricket. Of course, I know I made mistakes along the way, but I care passionately about the club – I always have done, and always will. Sometimes when I think about all that has gone on over all those years, I am reminded of a quote Margaret Thatcher made. 'If you believe passionately, you will always get opposition – so my life will always be uphill.'

CHAPTER 2

MY GREATEST CRICKETING REGRET

Like most cricket-mad young boys growing up in a mining community near Wakefield in the 1940s and 1950s, I dreamed of one day playing for Yorkshire and captaining the club. Whenever I went to my local nets or matches, Yorkshire cricket would be the only thing talked about. All I ever wanted was to play for Yorkshire. I didn't know if I would be good enough, but I had a dream, a dream that came true in 1962 when I made my debut.

I went on to play for them for the next 24 years until 1986 and captained the side for eight of those years from 1971 to 1978. I am proud to have followed in the footsteps of some great men who captained Yorkshire, but as I look back on my life I realise that taking on the role was the biggest mistake I ever made in my cricketing career. It led to countless arguments with the committee that diverted me from the main job of winning cricket matches, which was made hard enough by the inflated ambitions of other people, who had failed to realise times had changed.

The pressures and demands of captaining Yorkshire persuaded me to put my England career on hold for three years, losing possibly my best years in Test cricket, and I wonder what I would have achieved in international cricket if I had chosen a different course. Yorkshire cricket has been the love of my life and, even though that relationship has hit the rocks many times, I have always answered its call, returning to the Yorkshire board ten years ago and, as we have seen, becoming club president in 2012.

Just as the presidency was an honour I could not turn down, it was the same 40 years earlier when the club offered me the captaincy. It was a fairytale come true for a young kid who spent his childhood looking up to the men who played cricket for their county. They were superstars in our community, held in high esteem and envied by young boys who wanted to emulate their feats. My heroes were men who had been born and bred in the same communities as me.

The world seemed much smaller in those days. Most of us didn't have television and home computers were many years in the future, so the only way you could find out what was going on in the cricket was by reading the morning and afternoon newspapers, and in the 1950s they were printed in London and Manchester. We read the northern editions, which had reporters dedicated to covering Yorkshire cricket and giving it plenty of space and back-page headlines. What happened there would be the big story every day in the summer months, and the northern papers gave it the prominence the national press now reserves for the England team, so it is no surprise I one day wanted to wear the white rose.

I was lucky that I spent my formative years as a county player under the captaincy of Brian Close, studying his methods and learning something new every day. As a youngster I would field at third man, and not just stand there bored to death. I would watch and try to work out why he made certain decisions. Did they work? If so, why? I studied the way he changed the bowling. Why did Fred Trueman bowl only three overs this morning and then suddenly the spinners came on? Why did he keep moving the field placings? I noticed he was always shifting people around. I wasn't the only one to feel that. I remember one day when Dougie Padgett was fielding on the sweep. Closey said to him: 'Dougie, you are never in the right place.' To which he retorted: 'I have made that many new marks on the ground as you have shifted me, it is like noughts and crosses down here.'

I didn't just watch what he did, either. If I didn't understand why he had taken a certain decision, I would seek out Closey at teatime and ask him, not in an aggressive way, but just to quiz him so I could learn. I was a sponge taking it all in, because he was always active, trying to do something to help us win the game. Nothing was allowed to drift because he was so focused on victory. He was very patient with me, explaining why something would or would not work. It gave me a wonderful insight into how his mind clicked and the way he was thinking ahead. It was a perfect apprenticeship in Yorkshire cricket, and was one reason why I wanted to captain the club.

I learnt very early on that winning the County Championship

was the club's obsession, to the point that it was almost expected that we would win the title. This demand for success was understandable because for many years we had been bloody good at winning it. The official County Championship started in 1890 and in 69 years to 1968 (there was no County Championship during the two world wars), Yorkshire had won the title 30 times, way more than any other county.

As soon as I arrived in the Yorkshire first team in 1962, I quickly grasped it was almost an unspoken duty to carry on the traditions of the past. After a day's play when you were getting changed and chatting, the talk would be about how we were going to bowl out the opposition and get more points. It was all about winning.

In those days, every match was played on uncovered pitches, over three days. There were no questions about over-rates so time was your constant enemy, forcing the captain to think of innovative ways to win because you had to somehow ensure four innings were played in three days. Sides picked up a lot of points only if they won matches, with a few points available for a first-innings lead. This meant that while naturally you didn't want to lose, it was worth taking the risk to try to win.

It was only after my first season that official one-day cricket competitions began and we did not take limited-overs games seriously at Yorkshire. The Gillette Cup started in 1963 and was 65 overs per side. Six years later in 1969 the John Player Sunday League was introduced, followed by the Benson & Hedges Cup in 1972. This was not one-day cricket as we know it today, and we were not very good at it. When the John Player League started, Fred Trueman would bowl off a short run-up with two slips, then when someone cross-batted him over midwicket he used to think they were lucky beggars. We did not change our approach as we were still thinking in terms of three-day cricket. We did not have any nous or feel for the one-day game. For a side that played so well in championship cricket, we did not grasp how to play defensive, containing cricket. Given how attacking we were in the three-day game, it seems odd looking back that we couldn't make the switch.

Not for the first or last time in its history, Yorkshire were slow to change with the times. Others had stolen a march on us and were becoming very good at one-day cricket, particularly our big rivals Lancashire. They showed us up by winning the John Player League in 1969, and the following year they won the John Player League and the Gillette Cup. Their success put more pressure on Closey as captain, when the committee men realised the glory that could be associated with winning a one-day trophy. The Yorkshire public were fed up seeing Lancashire win cups, and at the end of the season in 1970 it was clear matters would come to a head. Closey had missed seven John Player League matches that year through injury, so there was little he could have done about our poor performances, but as usual the Yorkshire committee wanted someone to blame, and made him the scapegoat.

Aged 29 I was approaching my best years and wanted a stable environment at Yorkshire, not the uncertainty of playing under a new captain. At that time, Closey's vice-captain was the late Phil Sharpe and I knew there was a good chance of him being promoted to the captaincy because the committee liked posh amateurs. Phil had been to Worksop College, so he had the right schooling and the correct upbringing, but I did not rate him as a leader.

He was a nice guy but he was in the amateur mould, and he did not share my view of the game. I got the impression that his idea of county cricket was just to enjoy it. Each evening he would sit at the bar having beef sandwiches, a gin and tonic and if he got into a sing-song later on then all the better. He loved singing, when we played at Lord's or The Oval, along with Don Wilson he would often go to the Black & White Minstrel Show at the Victoria Palace in London. They were huge in those days, and often came into our dressing room to watch the cricket at Lord's and The Oval before heading off to the theatre for their show; Sharpe loved being around them. Well, I was more ambitious than that; I didn't just want to enjoy cricket, I wanted to win and to play for England.

Playing under that sort of person did not appeal to me at all, so before I flew to Australia that winter for the Ashes tour, I went to Closey's house. It was the only time I ever visited him there. The house was called, appropriately enough, High Places and I asked Brian if he was going to resign or retire. I wanted to know because I had to seriously think about my position and where it left me if he did decide to step down.

He gave me an absolute assurance he was not retiring and was loving the job. He was sure that the shoulder injury which had restricted him in 1970 would heal over the winter and he would be fine, so I went to Australia with a clear mind because I felt Yorkshire would be in safe hands with Brian staying in charge. I could go to Australia, concentrate on scoring runs for England and not worry about the politics and upheaval at Headingley. How wrong I was.

On the tour I batted well. I scored three centuries in the first four tour matches, but before the first Test in Brisbane John

Nash, the Yorkshire secretary, phoned me at 8.30pm in the evening and said that Close had resigned and the committee had voted unanimously to invite me to be captain. I was so surprised Closey had resigned, but chuffed to bits I had been offered the captaincy. The English media covering the tour wanted to speak to me so we held a press conference the following day.

It was then they told me Closey had been sacked. I was dumbfounded, totally speechless. I felt embarrassed because I had accepted the job thinking Brian had resigned. Later on I found out what actually happened: I had been elected captain by a majority vote, after it came down to either Don Wilson, the left-arm spinner, or me. The chairman then asked the committee if they could all vote again and make it look good, by nobody voting for Don this time so it would be carried through 'unanimously'. What duplicity and farce! It was a sign of things to come. So it was that my captaincy started with the club being economical with the truth, but that should not surprise anyone, seeing how Yorkshire was run in those days and what would unfold in the future.

While all this was going on, I was busy batting for England and was in the form of my life as we won the Ashes. Going into the final Test, I needed 18 runs to break Wally Hammond's all-time record of runscoring for a tour to Australia, but I broke my arm on a bad pitch at Sydney against Western Australia just before the seventh Test. Graham McKenzie's first ball hit me in the chest from just short of a length, the second ball nearly took my head off and the third ball hit me just above the left wrist in front of my face as I tried to protect myself. I went off to hospital and that was me finished. Even though it was a painful end, it had still been a fantastic tour and I had put Yorkshire to the back of my mind.

In time I returned home full of enthusiasm for the new job and could not wait to get started. I had a naive, boyish belief we were on the verge of great things, but I had failed to grasp two important factors. The first was that the great Yorkshire team of the 1960s had been broken up as players aged and moved on, but new talent had not been nurtured by the club, so the youngsters coming through struggled to live up to the standards we had set in the past. Throughout Yorkshire's history, the committee had not been known for its visionary approach. They just assumed that because Yorkshire had been fantastic in the past, and the county was full of kids wanting to play cricket, everything would be okay. They thought it would continue forever and we had a divine right to be top dog.

However, Closey had been sacked, Ray Illingworth had been forced out in 1968, and Fred Trueman retired in 1969 with keeper Jimmy Binks. Ken Taylor and Bryan Stott had gone as well. So it was that a side that had won seven championships between 1959 and 1968 and two Gillette Cups in 1965 and 1969 was now consigned to history. We were starting a new era, but were ill-equipped to keep up with other counties.

The second factor was overseas players were becoming a real force in the county game, making teams that Yorkshire had beaten in the past a lot tougher to play. All of a sudden when we came up against a team like Worcestershire, who we used to beat comfortably, we faced Glenn Turner, Ron Headley and Vanburn Holder. Nottinghamshire had Garfield Sobers, at the time the best player in the world. Lancashire could pick Clive Lloyd and Farokh Engineer. Warwickshire had Rohan Kanhai in his pomp and Lance Gibbs. Even smaller counties such as Glamorgan had Majid Khan and Gloucestershire Mike Procter. Kent were another exceptional side. They had John Shepherd and Bernard Julien from the West Indies as well as Asif Iqbal from Pakistan. The result was that Lancashire and Kent were dominating one-day cricket. English players were also starting to move counties much more frequently and the game was evolving but we were stuck in a time warp.

By contrast, in order to be able to play for Yorkshire, you had to be born in Yorkshire, which when I was a young kid made it feel as though you were already part of a special club, but now it meant the county was being held back. Talent is vital and once we entered a barren phase our opportunities for rebuilding the side were limited by geographical boundaries put in place many years before. A few players in the past had tried it on and lied about where they were born, but when the club found out they were shown the door, regardless of how good that player was. It was an unbreakable rule. Nowadays it would contravene countless European Union employment laws and a player would take the club to court winning a load of compensation money for discrimination.

Rightly it has now been consigned to history and we have moved on, extending a Yorkshire welcome to players from all over the world, which started when Sachin Tendulkar became our first overseas player in 1992. More than 20 years later, we have had players from almost every nation playing for us and have even been captained by an Australian, Darren Lehmann, in 2002.

But for me as captain in the 1970s, the rules were in place and I had to make the best of it. It was a nightmare trying to convince the ex-players on the cricket committee to think differently. These men had played in Championship-winning teams and could not comprehend change and would not accept that county cricket had moved on. They wanted us to remain a club that was made up of Yorkshiremen but still beat teams boasting players from all over the world. It was an impossible task.

I was lucky I had some fantastic kids in the team. The late David Bairstow, one of my best friends, was never down for more than five seconds. He had such positivity, exuberance and an energy that was uplifting for everybody in the side. I have not known anyone like him in my life. If I had to pick an all-time XI then Alan Knott would be my wicketkeeper, but I would make David twelfth man. In his playing days, his cup was always half full. It was a fantastic trait to be like that and such a tragedy that he later went on to take his own life.

Graham Stevenson, who died earlier this year, aged just 58, was talented but funny as well. Nobody has ever made me laugh as much as he did, he even made the umpires laugh. He also made me swear at him because he was daft as a brush, which in Yorkshire vernacular is said with affection. Setting fields for him sometimes was an art form in itself. He would be late every bloody day, but what a cricketer! The players would not go out for dinner or for a drink without Graham, they never allowed him a quiet night in.

Another key player in my squad was Arnie Sidebottom (father of Ryan), who played 16 games for Manchester United's first team at centre half. He was the best professional I ever played with. If I asked him to turn up at a certain time, he would be there ten minutes early. Ask him to bowl or bat and he would give you everything. He had reddish hair and he would go bright red in the sun on hot days. After one particularly hot day, Graham said to him: 'You look like my red setter.' So his nickname from then on was Red Dog. Phil Carrick, God rest his soul because cancer claimed him far too early, was such an even-natured man.

The good thing about those four kids was that it was a delight to play with them and yet they were also honest. If I came back in, having been given out lbw and questioned the decision, they would say: 'Well, you didn't get right forward.' They were not frightened of me, and they told me the truth. They were lovely guys who gave the side so much.

However, while they were all first-rate county players, we had one or two who weren't quite as good. For example, there was Peter Squires, who played left wing for England at rugby union. He was a brilliant fielder and a wonderful lad to play with, but he wasn't quite as strong a cricketer as the others. You can have great people, but you need to have a lot of talent as well. How do you compete against counties with three great overseas players? It was impossible.

I was also naive about the complexities of the job. The role of captain of Yorkshire was all-encompassing and not just about choosing which bowler to bowl at which end. You had to run the side on the field and organise things off it without any help. It was not like today, when even county sides have a vast array of backroom staff to help the captain. Instead, we had a physio, a scorer and that was it – the captain had to organise everything else.

When Closey was captain on away trips, he was handed a cheque by the secretary to cover our wages. He had to go to the bank when it opened at ten o'clock on the morning of the match and cash the cheque. He was given some brown envelopes with our names on and how much we should be paid, less the tax, and he would fill them with the money from the bank. He would count it out and give it to us before play started and then at 11.30am have to switch on and start thinking about the game. It was amazing the amount of peripheral nonsense he had to do.

During a home Championship match, Yorkshire would have a selection committee meeting for the next few games, with Brian Sellers, the chairman, calling the shots. Sellers would call Closey off the field and summon him into the meeting. While he was in the meeting, whoever was senior pro, for example Fred or Illy, would take over captaincy on the field. When Closey came back on the field, he would tell the senior pro to stay in charge for a few overs until he got the feel of what had been happening.

To make the whole situation worse, he still had no idea of the team that was being picked for the next match. The lads would ask him what had happened and who had been picked, but the committee would just ask Brian his opinion and then dismiss him while they made the decisions. Only at tea time did Mr Nash, the secretary, come in and give us the team news for the next three matches. It was a ridiculous way of doing things, and I would not stand for that as captain. I made myself unpopular with the committee because I told them so.

These people had been all-powerful for years but here was an upstart as a captain, a star for England, who was not prepared to accept the status quo. I thought my argument was reasonable and right, and that I had won them over by saying it can't be right to bring a captain off in the middle of a match when he was trying to win the game. I also pointed out that I was the only county captain not on the cricket and selection committee and spoke out strongly about this. I wanted a say and a vote on the team I was expected to take out on the field. It took time but eventually they agreed. I also told them I was not prepared to hand out the wage packets and suggested the secretary should do that.

Looking back, I can see why I put some backs up, but at that time they did not want to pick a fight with me because when Closey was sacked, the members had risen up in revolt. They had played merry hell with the committee, there had been petitions and groups formed calling for some committee men to resign. It was a little taste of what would happen subsequently when they also sacked me as captain. The members were angry with the committee over Brian's sacking and that winter Sellers, a former captain who was an autocratic leader, stood down as chairman of the cricket and selection committees to appease the members. However, nothing really changed because he stayed on the general committee, where he was able to still rule the club with an iron fist.

The new chairman of the committee was a weak, malleable man in John Temple, a nice guy who was popular and the perfect character to calm the storm. The peace was short lived, as I soon raised another issue with them where Yorkshire seemed to be operating in a very old-fashioned way. When I took over the captaincy, there were no fixed-term contracts for the players, and I'd seen the difficulties this caused for Closey and Illy. So I put it to the committee that we should have proper deals in place, which made me even more unpopular with them.

The situation was this: Yorkshire gave players a yearly agreement, starting on 1 August and running until the end of July the following year. Why it started in the middle of the summer season is anybody's guess. There was absolutely no sense in that arrangement. When a player was first signed up, the club wrote to him and said it would employ him for a year and specified the salary it would pay him. It was also agreed that the committee would let him know by the end of July whether he was being retained for a further year. This meant there was absolutely no security for players, who feared that a drop in form or a bit of bad luck with injuries could cost them their livelihood. To have that hanging over a player in the middle of a season was not a way to get the best out of them.

In those days, of course, cricketers did not earn very much money and there were no agents to find them commercial deals. Even senior players suffered under this system. In 1968, when Ray Illingworth asked for a three-year contract to have a bit of security late in his career, he was refused. Brian Sellers said to him: 'If you want to go, then you can fucking well go. Fuck off.' He actually used those words. So Illy went, joined Leicestershire and won trophies. His life was all the better because he left Yorkshire and earned himself a decent contract.

It was a ridiculous situation, and I knew I had to address this issue because it was causing so much trouble in the dressing room. Tony Nicholson, the fast bowler and another man who died too young, helped me because he was good at buttering up the committee men at the bar. Between us, we also squeezed more money out of them for the players. But it did not do me any good standing up for the team, as the committee resented me for it.

There were some good men among the 23 on the general committee, but most of them were weak. I do not say that with nastiness; they just did not want to challenge the cricket committee, which was mainly made up of ex-players. Many on the general committee would look up to them, as former stars of Yorkshire, and believed that they would know what they were talking about when it came to cricket and what cricketers wanted. After all, they'd been there themselves, so surely their opinions had to carry more weight. Non-cricket people often find it hard to speak out against men who have perhaps been brilliant at cricket in their lifetime. How do you convince people like Brian Sellers, who had been amateur captain of Yorkshire, that he is wrong? Herbert Sutcliffe was another on the cricket committee, he was a great player. And then there was Don Brennan, who had also played for England. These guys were not bad men but they were stuck in their ways, and they did not realise that the game had moved on since their day.

As the team became poorer in ability the harder I tried and the better I batted but it made no difference, we were just not good enough. So when Yorkshire wanted someone to blame, they decided to point the finger at me. I accept we did not play very well. We finished 13th in the Championship in my first year and won just four matches, though incidentally I made runs in all of those wins. I averaged 109.85 that season and I gave the team everything as I tried to lead from the front. Things were no better in the John Player League, where we finished 16th, winning just five games and losing nine. We had not made any progress from Closey's last year.

That is when all the backbiting started. Whenever I went to

a cricket committee meeting there were complaints. The same thing would happen at selection meetings, and it became fashionable to blame me for all the problems. When I left Yorkshire to play for England, my back was turned and there were plenty of trouble-makers willing to slip a knife between my shoulder blades. The more runs I scored, the more the team failed and some people tried to match the two events as if they were linked in some way. Yorkshire had become a one-man team and I was accused of being obsessed with my own scores. The facts speak for themselves, though, and there was no escaping the simple truth that we needed an injection of new blood, but Sellers had been burnt by the sacking of Close and was not about to rock the boat by ripping away years of tradition to sign overseas players.

In 1972 we improved, in one-day cricket at least, peaking in a Benson & Hedges Cup semi-final win over Gloucestershire at Headingley. They had Mike Procter in the team, who was one of the world's star all-rounders at the time. I read the pitch well and realised we needed five seamers, so I put them in to bat. We bowled them out for 131 in 55 overs. I knew the only way they could win was if Procter and Jack Davey, a good left-arm seamer, took early wickets, because it was likely to seam around all day.

So I defended against those two, kept my wicket intact and waited to score off the three other bowlers. While I was winning the match, not looking to play shots but stay in, one or two in the crowd started to shout out. They had no idea of the pitch and thought we should knock off 131 quickly. One guy shouted out in support of me: 'Whatever thou does Geoff, they will sack thee.' How prophetic. I was man of the match, and scored 75 not out as we won by seven wickets. We'd nullified their threats, as Procter took none for 34, Davey bowled nine overs taking one for six.

We were favourites to win the final because of my form, but on 5 July in the first round of the Gillette Cup at Headingley, Bob Willis hit me on the finger, splitting it open, and I had to be rushed to hospital, given an injection and put to sleep so they could operate. It was like a squashed tomato and I missed the Benson & Hedges final. If I had made 30 or 40 runs, we might have won it but Leicestershire, captained by Ray Illingworth, beat us, so then I got the blame for not playing with a load of stitches holding my finger together.

The opposition was in full swing now, with Richard Hutton the chief protagonist. At one point, he tried to organise a letter to be sent to the committee expressing a lack of faith in my ability. The players refused to sign and it fell through. My relationship with Don Wilson was also strained and he seemed obstructive towards much that I tried to do. It felt like I was batting with a sack of coal on my back; the burden got heavier and heavier and weighed me down.

Of course there were things I could have done better; I hold my hands up. I wasn't a good man-manager, I accept that. I was a strong-minded individual, so I tackled the committee about things and answered them back where perhaps I could have been more diplomatic. I took on senior players, so should not have been surprised when the whispering campaign against me began. When that happens it erodes trust and quite honestly my nature would not allow me to give in and admit failure and defeat. The determination to succeed and tenacity that helped me bat in the toughest situations was, in this case, my undoing.

Remaining captain in that atmosphere was such a mistake. The job brought me so much pain and trouble. It wasted so much time and energy, which I could and should have put to better use by pouring it into my batting, I just did not have the brains to pack it in. I should have learnt from history. Herbert Sutcliffe had the foresight to avoid the job and the strain that came with it. In 1927, he was offered the captaincy but turned it down because he knew it was the era of the amateur captain and it would be a burden and distract him from his batting. He was smart; I was not.

The guy who had best of both worlds was Len Hutton. When he became the first professional captain of England and went to Australia in 1954–55, he just had five Test matches to worry about. There was no media intrusion, no interviews about your personal life, no press conferences at the end of each day. Cricket writers wrote about the cricket. There was a manager on tour who handled everything off the field. In England, he would play five Tests as captain, but in between he would go back to Yorkshire, play under amateur captain Norman Yardley and just bat without any pressure. It must have been a lovely respite for him.

He had the status of being England captain but no outside problems of handling a committee and the politics of Yorkshire. Years later, Len spoke about me as captain of Yorkshire and spotted the difference between my era and his. He clocked the media in my day were far more dogged and summed it up in Alan Hill's book on Herbert Sutcliffe entitled *Cricket Maestro*. Hill wrote that Leonard had told him I was a 'prisoner of circumstances'. That was a very interesting and astute judgement.

It made no difference how many runs I made, the team were just not good enough. I loved the challenge of tactics, changing the bowling and field placings, I had the mind for those aspects of the job. Man-management, diplomacy and PR were not my strong suits.

I was not a political animal; I could not toady up to the committee men, pour drinks down their necks at the bar and make them feel important. I was too focused on the cricket. Alcohol and pubs were a big thing in cricket then. Everybody would go to the bar every night, but I didn't. I remember the first time I played for Yorkshire seconds, Brian Sellers came to the match and bought everyone a drink, even the kids would have a beer. When asked, I said: 'I would like an orange juice, please.' He replied: 'If you want an orange juice, you can buy your own bloody drink.' That was the culture. Brian was not a bad man, but he thought if you had a drink it would solve everything. It was a very macho approach.

My Uncle Algy got it right years ago. He used to say: 'Buy them a couple of drinks and they are on your side forever.' I was not made like that, but I was not smart enough to see I was fighting a losing battle.

It was no surprise that the plotting behind my back happened in a pub. They staged their meetings at the Half Moon in Collingham, north of Leeds, which is ironic because now I pass it on my way home from Headingley to my new house in Boston Spa. This was where the committee plotted to get rid of me as captain and stuck knives in my back. They thought it was a secret, but what they didn't know was that Terry Brindle, who was the cricket writer on the *Yorkshire Post* through the 1970s and 1980s, lived in Wetherby four miles away and often went to drink there. They tried to get him in their camp to write bad stuff about me, but he refused.

Among those who met there to try to get me deposed were Don Brennan, a real wannabe who lived in the past; he was a former England wicketkeeper full of strong opinions. Then there was Captain Desmond Bailey from Middlesbrough, who was all port and hot air. Harry McIlvenny, Brian Sellers, Billy Sutcliffe (son of Herbert) were all also involved. Terry Brindle would humour them, so they thought he was on their side but would then tell me what was going on, hence I was far better informed than they thought.

My mind became so frazzled by the end of the 1974 season that I decided the thing to do was give up playing for England and concentrate on Yorkshire. I felt the only way to succeed was to captain and play every match for Yorkshire. Without my runs they were poor and I could not serve two masters at once. I issued a press statement at the time saying I was going to stay in Yorkshire and find out who my true friends were (I did not say and I would also find out who my foes were).

Having recently met Rachael, the other love of my life, the next season was one of the happiest times I spent at Yorkshire as we managed to come second in the Championship, which was a great achievement with the young team I had. That kept my detractors at bay for a while, but it did not last and for three years between 1974 and 1977 I played only county cricket, which was far too long away from the international scene.

During the time I didn't play for England, they were losing Test matches and the Yorkshire committee were telling me that I should be batting for my country. Then, when I decided to make myself available to play for England again in 1977 and

Yorkshire lost a couple of matches in my absence, they criticised me for not being there. What was I supposed to do: cut myself in half and give one bit to Yorkshire, the other to England? That is how stupid the situation had become by the end. It was a no-win situation, but I would not let the captaincy go until they finally sacked me. How foolish was I?

I am sure I would have played with more freedom and scored more runs in the 1970s if I had never captained Yorkshire. Don't get me wrong, I always loved the Yorkshire members and was passionate about playing for the county, but the people who were running the club made it at times unbearable for me. The rulers had a history of doing what they wanted and sacking players seemingly on a whim. The only difference with me was the members were finally sick of their petty jealousies and decided enough was enough and toppled the committee after I was sacked as a player in 1983.

It is ironic that they blamed me for the uprising. 'Boycott caused all the trouble,' they say, as if I could have canvassed all those people personally to take a stand in 1983. Nonsense! The committee were the ones with the power to make the decisions, not me. They started the unrest, they did the sackings and they reaped what they sowed. They were the ones who underestimated the members, and forgot it was a members' cricket club and not a private gentleman's club run for their own gratification. Sadly, in all the years since, not once have I ever heard one of those committee men say they were in the wrong.

CHAPTER 3

MY WORLD COMES CRASHING DOWN

My nightmare began on Wednesday 14 August 2002 with an everyday event: I was having a shave.

I felt fit and healthy, and only two days previously had been working at Trent Bridge for ESPN television commentating on a Test match between England and India. My television career was going well and, for the first time in my life, I was about to get married, having become engaged to Rachael on her 50th birthday the previous May. But that August evening at the Atlantic Hotel in Jersey it all changed.

I had flown over because one of my best friends, David Falle, had asked me if I would speak on the Wednesday evening at the Royal Jersey Golf Club. I was getting ready for the dinner and had a shave. While stretching the skin on the left side of my neck, I noticed it seemed to feel unusually firm, and something was just not right. I kept poking around but couldn't find anything specific to cause concern. My health was good, I did not feel ill and had no symptoms other than this baffling firmness. I even began to wonder if it had always been like that and I'd somehow never noticed. However, I knew it hadn't been there when I shaved that morning.

I went to the dinner, and when I came back I had another look at my neck: it was still hard. The following morning I did the same thing and whenever I went back to my room that day I would check again, and it was still firm. It was puzzling and a bit worrying, because I knew that if you found a small lump or unusual swelling the advice was always to go straight to the doctor.

After a day and a half of poking around, I went to a doctor in Jersey; he had a look at me, was not happy and told me I needed to see a specialist as soon as I got back to Yorkshire. When I flew home on the Sunday, I decided to put my fears to one side and not tell Rachael or our young daughter Emma about the lump. I didn't want to worry them, especially as the next day we were due to host a special lunch at our house in Woolley for the Indian cricket team.

I had been doing a lot of commentary in India at the time, so I'd got to know the Indian lads well, and some of them had asked me if they could visit my house when they came to England. They had seen pictures of this old farmhouse with lots of greenery, a six-foot waterfall in the garden and all this space, which they do not get much of in the Indian cities. So I said yes, but I was not going to go to a lot of trouble unless it was put in their official Tour itinerary, as I wanted to be sure they would definitely turn up. The lunch was kept very private, and the whole team came, along with coach John Wright, the team manager, physio and even the bus driver. I invited only eight close friends: Richard and Allison Knaggs, Tracy and Alison Jackson, Malcolm Guy, and Janet Bairstow with her two young children, Jonny and Becky, as well as one very special friend, an Indian reporter called Debu Datta.

Thinking our Indian guests would like some familiar food, Rachael had organised the Aagrah Restaurant to come to the house and cook for them (in fact, Sachin Tendulkar said he would just love a steak). It was only when they arrived that she realised, after Emma told her, that the Aagrah chain of restaurants is Pakistani and not Indian. She was slightly embarrassed and joked that they might 'nobble' the Indian team, Pakistan's fiercest rivals, before their match against England. However, she need not have worried as the food was excellent. The chef and all the waiters were more interested in being in Geoffrey Boycott's house and having photographs with me, than seeing or meeting any of the Indian cricket team.

The chance to talk about cricket with the Indian lads helped take my mind off my personal worry. It was a gorgeous sunny day, and Emma and the Bairstow kids organised a putting contest on my golf green – she even lent the young 17-year-old wicketkeeper Pathiv Patel her left-handed putter. My good friends Sourav Ganguly, VVS Laxman and Rahul Dravid wanted to watch films of me batting and insisted Rachael find some old videos and put them on, while I sat down with Sachin, who had asked if he could have a private chat about his batting.

After that we went into my conservatory to talk to the seam bowlers and I told them: 'Look, you can't win this Test match if you go on bowling like you have been [England had scored

487 and 617 in their first innings in the first two Tests]. Wickets are costing you over forty runs per wicket, and let me tell you at Headingley there are no draws – you either win or lose! Get it into your head: be positive about winning. If you bowl like you are, you will not win; you have to bowl a more disciplined line around off stump.'

I asked Sachin how they could win with this bowling. He said: 'Geoffrey, you are right. I had never thought about it like that; we would need nine hundred runs.'

I then went through all the England players and told them where to bowl. I don't know if this chat made a difference, but it helped me at a time when I was very worried about my throat. It was marvellous to see Sachin go on to score 193 and they won the Headingley Test by an innings and 46 runs, having lost the first Test at Lord's and drawn the second one at Trent Bridge. Before anyone accuses me of not being supportive of the England team and of being unpatriotic, they didn't ask me for any help. If any player of any nationality asks me for help, I give it gladly because lots of people gave me free advice and help throughout my career if I approached them.

The next day, I went to my local GP to obtain a referral to see an ear, nose and throat specialist. On my return home I got into a trivial argument with Rachael; she was standing at the kitchen sink at the time and accused me of being very 'tetchy' with her. When she said that, I just blurted out the reason I had been to see the doctor: I had something wrong with the side of my neck and he had referred me to a specialist the next afternoon. Fortunately, Emma was not present at the time and we decided to keep our worries from her until we knew more information, but I was already really concerned.

I still had a very busy diary, and first thing the next day I was due to go to Headingley, as Fred Trueman, Brian Close, Ray Illingworth and I were jointly opening the East Stand. Once again I had to appear normal and smile for the cameras. I didn't speak to anybody about my cancer fears, although it was a relief that I now had Rachael in my confidence.

After the ceremony I went to see the ENT specialist, Ian Fraser, who had very kindly agreed to see me at his home near Harrogate, and he arranged for me to have an ultrasound later that week. In the meantime, I had to put everything to the back of my mind again as we had arranged a dinner that night at our house for my ESPN colleagues Sunil Gavaskar, Ravi Shastri, Harsha Bhogle, Navjot Sidhu (the mad Sikh who I love dearly), and Alan Wilkins, the former Glamorgan player. ESPN boss Huw Bevan was also there, as we chatted and looked ahead to the Test starting the next day on the Thursday. This time Rachael cooked steak and kidney pie and they all loved it.

I mentioned to Huw, nobody else, that I needed to get away on the Friday of the Test match for a 1.30pm medical appointment. I did not go into details or tell him it was for an ultrasound at Roundhay Hospital in Leeds. But at that appointment they told me they had found a small node in my neck, and tried to reassure me by saying it could be one of a number of things. I just sensed that was not good news. However, I could not dwell on it as I needed to immediately return back to commentating on the Test match.

I thought I had kept it a secret, but the next day when I got home from commentating at Headingley there was a message on my answering machine from Fred Trueman, who worked for the *Sunday People* newspaper, asking me what was wrong with my throat as he'd heard there was a story coming out the next day.

A colleague in the media then telephoned that evening and asked if there was any truth in me having cancer because it was going to be in the Sunday papers. Apparently someone had recognised me at Roundhay Hospital, asked a member of staff what was I doing there and they had been told I had throat cancer! I was very angry. Some sections of the press really are unbelievable. The news was out there that I definitely had cancer; not that I maybe had cancer or that I was just having tests. No, according to the papers Geoffrey Boycott had cancer. In their rush to get a 'scoop' they did not even think to ask me; they did not give it a thought that maybe no actual diagnosis had been made by the doctors and I had been told it could be harmless or a benign lump.

Our daughter had gone to stay at her grandma's in Whitby, so Rachael had to ring her mum and Emma to explain that a story was going to appear in the papers the next day but that it may not be true, and I was just having tests so hopefully would be fine. Emma was only 13 at the time and we should have been allowed to protect her, and to have told her in our own way. Thank goodness Fred thought to warn us of the pending story and she did not have to see it first in the Sunday papers. It would have been a horrible way for her to learn about my possible illness. I phoned Fred later to thank him for tipping me off. Rachael then spent the rest of the night ringing other family members and close friends, explaining that it still might be nothing at all and the reason we had not said anything was there didn't seem any point in worrying people unnecessarily.

Next day all hell broke loose, there were press men everywhere when I arrived at Headingley for the fourth day of the Test. The secretary of Yorkshire said there were journalists and photographers asking for extra passes to the game, but he had refused most of them and told them to pay at the gate. I declined all approaches but could not stop them taking pictures of me. When I phoned the lady in charge at the hospital, Pat Oldfield, to complain and ask her to find out who had leaked the story, she was very apologetic and did later come back to say they couldn't find the culprit.

While I felt my diagnosis was not looking good at that stage, I had not been told I had cancer and there was still hope, yet here it was, all over the bloody national daily newspapers, telling me and the whole world I had throat cancer. I still don't know exactly how the press got hold of the story, but I suppose people do a lot of things for money or perhaps it was just loose talk.

My next appointment was for an x-ray on my chest on Wednesday 28 August at the Bupa Methley Hospital, which was clear, and provided a small piece of good news. I then went into the Bupa Roundhay Hospital two days later and stayed in overnight because they wanted to take out the lump and have it biopsied. It later turned out, when I went to see the oncologist she would have preferred them not to operate, as she was concerned that when they removed the lump any cancer cells left behind may have entered my blood stream – not exactly the kind of news you want to hear.

But it was too late, the operation had been performed and I just had to wait for the results. I tried to keep our minds off it all by taking Rachael to Old Trafford to watch Manchester United play Middlesbrough along with my best friend Richard

Knaggs on Tuesday 3 September. It was an evening match and we were having dinner before the game when the ENT specialist phoned my mobile and said: 'Look you had better come and see me tomorrow morning.' We knew then for sure it was not good.

Next morning my GP's nurse, Julie Huxley, took out the stitches on my neck from the operation and I then went to see Ian Fraser at the hospital at 12.30. He said they had found cancerous tissue in the biopsy. The news left me numb; it was the worst moment of all, because everyone knows that so many people die from cancer. I had known it was coming, but I still went very quiet. My mind started racing: What do I do now? What happens next?

When I got home, I phoned Huw Bevan and explained the diagnosis and said that I couldn't commentate at The Oval Test the following week. I knew that from then on I had to concentrate on the cancer and work out how the hell I was going to stay alive.

Initially I was consumed by fear, facing life and death decisions. Over the next few weeks I would experience the emotions of anger, confusion and desperation as I faced the greatest battle of my life. I was nearly 62 years old and had never smoked or been a drinker. I had never drunk spirits or even a pint of beer in my life, just the occasional glass of cinzano bianco with lots of lemonade or maybe a glass of champagne or wine, so I couldn't understand the diagnosis. Like everybody else faced with such a situation I was asking: Why me?

Without any discussions with Rachael, I not only cancelled my flights to Australia for the upcoming Ashes series but also my credit cards, memberships and annual subscriptions because I thought there was no point in looking to the future when I knew I could be dead.

It was Emma's 14th birthday on 5 September, so she came home that night from her grandma's house as we had previously organised a party for her the next day. She was also due to go back to her boarding school, after the long summer break, three days later on the Sunday. We had to explain to her that I did have cancer after all, and there were tears all round. It still breaks my heart just thinking about that moment. Having to tell this to my only child, especially at such a young age, is probably one of the hardest things I have ever had to do. It was all very distressing, and made me cry. I felt I had been given a death sentence.

Nowadays I am not ashamed to admit it, but at the time I was embarrassed, ashamed and upset because over the next days I would often go into a room on my own and break down in tears. A grown man crying, it was embarrassing and I would try to hide it, even from Rachael. It was so distressing, my mind was in turmoil and I could not think straight, my head was in a total spin. I was getting angry at myself because here I was breaking down all the time.

After a few days of this I had to tell myself: 'Listen, crying ain't going to make you better. If you just sit in a corner and keep crying you sure as hell are definitely going to die.' So I said to myself: 'What are you going to do about it? Pick yourself up and give it your best shot. Whatever it takes, be positive. This is ridiculous: I have always had patience, concentration and been mentally strong with my batting.'

On the Friday afternoon, Rachael and I saw Mr Fraser again and he accompanied us to meet Jamie Woodhead, the local cancer specialist at Cookridge Hospital in Leeds. Mr Woodhead said the tumour was about the size of an old six-pence coin, and he believed it was a secondary tumour and that the primary needed to be found which, if Rachael remembers correctly, he said could come from only one of three places: either behind the nose, in the palette or in the tongue.

I had all weekend to think about this and try to get used to the idea and on the Monday we returned for me to have an MRI and CT scan. Afterwards we met with Brendan Carey, the specialist who had read my results, and he said that I was lucky. (I did not know it then but 'lucky' was a word I was to hear a few times over the next months.) He told me I had two further secondary tumours in my shoulder and one in the neck but they had not spread to my body.

I asked why that was lucky, and he replied: 'If it spreads down in to your body, you have only a five per cent chance of survival.' I was stunned.

He also told me something quite revealing. He said the scans had shown that I have a baby spleen, which was about a quarter of the normal size, and he was quite puzzled by it. It was a shock to me as well. I explained that when I was eight, I'd had my spleen removed after rupturing it when falling off the railings in my back garden and landing on the upturned handle of an old mangle. During the night after the accident, while asleep, I had been bleeding internally and my life was saved only because my grandmother came to the house very early the next morning to see how I was. Recognising some-thing was wrong she insisted the doctor be sent for and I was rushed off to hospital to have an emergency operation to remove it.

Your spleen stores the antibodies that fight off infections and that is why I always had problems. In the 1960s and 1970s I was wary of going to play cricket in India, where conditions were harsh and infection a real danger. As Brendan Carey explained, the surgeon must have left behind a very small bit of my spleen after the operation and over the years it had grown, so I did have some, if not a lot, of protection after all.

It was not the only shock of the day. In the afternoon Rachael and I went to the Bupa Roundhay Hospital to see Mr Woodhead again who now, having studied my MRI test results, told me I had a tumour the size of a small orange at the base of my tongue.

Having been told I had a tumour about two centimetres wide, suddenly now I have one six centimetres wide; this was a big change. He said he needed to operate quickly and had a slot for surgery later that week. I remember sitting there thinking that a small orange seemed bloody big and feeling taken aback that it was in my tongue and not my neck. I'd had no symptoms, could not feel anything unusual on my tongue and had no idea how this had happened.

I was in a fog trying to get my head around it all and suddenly he wanted to operate immediately. In my confused state, I worried that if they could get the size of the tumour wrong once, they could get anything wrong. So I told him I needed to go home and have a bit of time to think about what I wanted to do. When I got back home I began searching round to get help and information, as it was a hell of a big call I was having to make.

I phoned Professor Ken McLennan on Saturday 14 September for some background information on tumours and what to do. Meanwhile, around this time, we were fortunate enough to start receiving books and magazines through the post from well-meaning people who had read in the newspapers about my cancer. I could not focus on them, but Rachael felt she needed to look at everything. Some books were from America and full of medical jargon, and they were not clear about what was best to actually do and she just flipped through those.

The one book that immediately stood out was called *Everything You Need to Know to Help You Beat Cancer*, written by Chris Woollams. It was a simple paperback, very easy to read and understand for anyone without medical knowledge or training. Most cancer books tell you what not to do; this was the opposite and told you what you should do. When she gave it to me, I couldn't concentrate long enough to fully understand what I was reading; I was dealing with too many emotions so Rachael went through the book again and highlighted the parts which she insisted I should read and from then on it became our bible. I spoke to Chris on the phone and he has been there for me ever since. Even now we occasionally have a catch-up.

The first thing he said when I got in touch was: 'Let's try to work out the cause.' He asked if I smoked or drank or used mouthwash, to which the answer to all three was no. So he then said the only thing he could think of was that I must have picked up a parasite while travelling somewhere like Sri Lanka, India, Pakistan or Bangladesh. Apparently a parasite can produce toxins and carcinogens that can cause inflammation in the gut, which in turn has an effect all around the body. He told me to take a course of ParaFree to kill any parasite and also to balance my gut bacteria with probiotics, as I could not get better until the bacteria were killed off. He then went on to tell me about milk thistle and a liver flush using Epsom salts and how I should take daily exercise.

Chris had only recently started to dedicate his life to researching cancer therapies and cures. His teenage daughter Catherine had been diagnosed with an incurable brain tumour and told the medical profession could do nothing for her. Not wanting to accept this, he used his skills and knowledge from his MA in biochemistry and set off all over the world researching a cure for her.

Miraculously, he managed to get her into remission for a time but unfortunately it returned in later years and sadly his daughter passed away. On the back of her initial recovery, Chris formed a charity, CANCERactive, and a monthly magazine called *Icon*. Chris's work and charity have gone from strength to strength since then, and he tells it very straight. He is not afraid of the big drug companies, who make fortunes out of producing cancer drugs, and he says many people are dying of ignorance not cancer. His philosophy is to arm you with as much information as possible, so that you are better able to make your own choices, because each person's cancer is different. He does not advocate alternative therapy, and his advice is designed to complement treatment from your oncologist, not replace it. I can honestly say Chris helped us more than any other person, and Rachael is convinced if she had not been able to keep falling back on his advice, I would be dead. I have to agree with her.

Chris has a 15-point checklist of what people should do when they discover they have cancer, and number one is to find a 'cancer buddy', someone close to you who can help take you to appointments, listen to the doctor's comments and advice (as you never take it all in), check your medicine and offer support during the dark times that inevitably follow once the treatment has started. He warned me that the punishing nature of chemotherapy and radiotherapy would leave me lifeless.

He said I would need a 'buddy' to help me get up in the mornings, cook my food and also try to ensure we lived a vestige of a normal life, my mind would be frazzled with the pain and discomfort and I would need a rock. For me that meant Rachael, I was lucky. Chris also emphasised the importance of home comforts in helping me to fight the disease. This turned out to be vital advice for me, because a few very well-meaning people had recommended different hospitals and doctors in places as varied as New York, Switzerland and London. But being treated at one of those hospitals would have required weeks renting an apartment or staying in a hotel having room service and being away from my family, friends and home life.

It would also have separated us from Emma, who was away at school in the week but came home most weekends. Her presence would be hugely uplifting and important to me during my months of treatment and she often helped her mother, not least of all by ganging up on me when I needed bullying! Living in a hotel and a strange environment would have added more stress to Rachael, who had so much on her plate already, and in those circumstances you do not want any additional worries.

Caring for someone with cancer, or any serious illness, is a tremendous burden and immensely stressful. I have nothing but admiration for people who dedicate their lives to looking after a loved one, sacrificing so much for the care of someone else. If that patient dies, they can often feel a sense of responsibility as if they failed in some way. Coping with the grief of loss is hard enough, but to think you failed a loved one in their hour of need must be unbearable, even if other people tell you that there was nothing more you could have done.

Rachael admits she knew from the beginning it was not going to be easy and felt quite emotional at the enormity of the task. She thought it was her responsibility to make sure I lived, not just for her and me, but for Emma's sake too. She believed that if I didn't make it, it would be her fault. So Chris's advice rang true straightaway and helped us decide to stay at home in Woolley.

One of the main things he also told me to do when I rang him was that it was imperative that I detoxed my whole body and change my way of eating. Changing my diet was no problem, but he also wanted me to have a coffee enema, which Rachael bought at the chemist as a DIY kit. She read out the instructions to me, and it was only then that I realised I had to shove it up my arse! She explained that I had to lie on the tiled bathroom floor, because it might make a mess, and that she would do it for me if I was not going to do it myself. I said to her: 'You ain't shoving anything up my arse!' The idea was dropped. It was the only piece of advice Chris gave us that I didn't follow – and I'm bloody glad I didn't.

Rachael had already been contacted by Sarah Surety, a feng shui lady we knew, and she too had mentioned the importance of detoxing and she also knew a nutritionist not too far away, Stacey Darrell, who could help. So I rang Stacey and she travelled from her home in Pickering, North Yorkshire, and stayed with us for three days and two nights to go through everything and show Rachael what foods to cook and what to throw out of the cupboards. She made me eat only miso soup for two days and drink lots of water, but this had to come from a glass bottle as nothing stored in plastic was allowed.

She left her menu book with instructions I could have lots of vegetables cooked a certain way, brown rice with tahini (sesame paste) and eventually I would be allowed white fish or chicken but no red meat or any dairy products. Everything had to be freshly prepared and organic where possible, with no ready meals allowed. Rachael had to get a soya margarine called Pure and use only a natural fruit sugar in my food. She got some oat milk in the end, because soya milk was just too sickly for her, as she had joined in eating the same things I did, in order to support me.

A friend of mine suggested I start taking a tablet called Revenol (an antioxidant) and put me in touch with Caroline Carey, who was an agent for a company called Neways which sells complementary therapies and treatments. Caroline suggested I also chew some apricot kernels, which contain the natural compound amygdalin (or B17), as they are believed to aid cancer treatment.

I asked Chris Woollams for his take on this and he confirmed the Revenol helped stop inflammation, among other things, and he explained how to take the apricot kernels. Apparently they can be helpful to some people, but he warned that I should never chew more than five or six in any 90-minute period, with a maximum of about 35 a day. I had to be careful because they contain cyanide, and people with cancer also have liver problems so I would need watching. If I turned a bit yellow or grey then I had to stop taking them. He also advised me to increase my intake gradually each day, starting with only five a day.

Later on, when my cancer treatments were decided by the oncologist, Chris drove up to see me. He built a programme of supplements for me – antioxidants mainly – that I should start taking before and after the chemotherapy. When it was time for my radiation, I had different tablets before and after as recommended by him. Among others he suggested fish oils and curcumin, which is derived from turmeric, to stop inflammation. I liked his honesty about what to do and was grateful because he did not try to fool me with empty promises. Nobody can give you guarantees when facing cancer.

Over the weekend of 14 September friends who had survived cancer were in touch offering advice. Paul Sykes, who built the Meadowhall shopping centre in Sheffield, came to see me and told me he went to the Johns Hopkins Hospital in Baltimore in the USA, for prostate cancer treatment. Because of the superb experience he had there, he donated millions of pounds for a new cancer wing at St James's University Hospital in Leeds, which was being built to replace the old ramshackle Cookridge Hospital I attended.

Another friend of mine, Russell Homer from Jersey, said he could put me in touch with John Watkinson at Queen Elizabeth Hospital in Birmingham, who is a specialist in cancer of the thyroid and he would be happy to give me advice and help, so I spoke to him. He was very positive and confident. He asked if I minded him making some enquiries on my behalf at the Cookridge Hospital. I was like a sponge soaking all this up, I wanted as much information as possible. When John got back in touch, he said he had learnt the operation would take eight hours. He said the surgeon would have to break my jaw in order for him to be able to remove the tumour, then my jaw would be re-wired shut for it to heal and I would not be able to talk for six weeks. As Rachael kindly pointed out, not talking for six weeks would be a problem for me especially!

He went on to say his information was that Mr Woodhead had been in the job for only a year and, while he was very good, it was doubtful he had done this operation before. Apparently the cancer specialist who had been his predecessor for a lot of years had just recently died himself from a brain tumour.

This information threw me into doubt about whether or not to have the operation. The clincher for me was when I asked John what he would do in my position, he replied he would not have the operation. He said there were only three surgeons in the UK he would want to operate on him to treat this type of cancer. One of them was Professor Pat Bradley, who worked only for the NHS at Nottingham General Hospital and was also the chairman of the British Association of Head and Neck Surgeons. John agreed to phone Pat Bradley on my behalf on the Sunday, and an appointment was set up for a consultation at 2pm on Tuesday 17 September in Nottingham. He would then perform the exploratory operation first thing the next morning. Pat said he wanted to knock me out and have a look down my throat himself, in order to be satisfied exactly where and how big my tumour was.

On Monday 16 September, Rachael and I attended the oncologists' clinic at Cookridge Hospital at 9.30am, meeting my oncologist Catherine Coyle for the first time. Jamie Woodhead, the surgeon, was also there. I told them I had decided to seek a second opinion and was going down to Nottingham the next day to see Pat Bradley.

It's about an hour's journey down to Nottingham from Woolley and Rachael insisted she drive as I couldn't concentrate on anything. Pat's a gregarious Irishman and he made me laugh when I joked with him that he'd better not have any Guinness that night if he was operating on me the following morning. He reassured me he did his best surgery the day after having a few drinks the night before to relax him. Rachael and I went to stay in a hotel that night, as we had to arrive back very early next morning for my operation as Pat was doing me a big favour by fitting me into his busy schedule, but neither of us really got any sleep.

That morning, I went down to theatre and Pat took nine biopsies and had a good look around. He then came to see me in my hospital bed a couple of hours later and told me straight-away I had a tumour as big as a 50 pence piece. He also said it was too large and too close to my voice box for him to guarantee, if he operated to remove it, that I would not lose my speech. He explained he would need to take out a larger area than just the tumour to make sure of removing all the cancer cells.

If the worst scenario happened during the operation, then obviously my quality of life would suffer as I would not be able to speak. He said I was lucky because the tumour was on the left side of my tongue and not across the mid-line. Apparently that was important because the blood supply for the tongue is down the middle. If any tumour goes across it, then they have to cut out the tongue because it would never heal and would just be dead meat in the mouth. He said he would operate if I wanted him to, but his recommendation was I have chemo-therapy and radiation treatment instead of surgery. He added that, because I had not smoked or been a regular drinker of alcohol in my life, my chances of success with chemotherapy and radiations were nearly as good as having surgery.

He warned me that the tumour was now so big I would need to decide quickly. He also mentioned that once they operated they could not then go back to chemotherapy and laser treat-ments; I had to choose either one or the other. I asked him what would happen if I did nothing. He replied: 'I give you three months.' In other words, I would be dead just after Christmas.

I can tell you that being given three months to live is a real showstopper. I remember he also looked Rachael straight in the eye and said: 'You will be surprised how many wives of very successful men can't cope with their partner's cancer and are not still with them at the end of it all; Geoffrey will need your help.'

I did not really grasp what he was saying, but Rachael knew immediately that he was warning her it was not going to be easy, that it was going to be tough on her too, not just me. Pat said he knew my oncologist in Leeds and would send her his report and I must then decide what I was going to do. When Rachael eventually drove me home, we travelled pretty much in silence as we were both a bit numb at what we had heard and at the enormity of the decision we were facing.

Out of the blue on the next day, a Macmillan nurse, Julie Hoole, called at the house. We were baffled as we did not know she was coming or anything about what Macmillan stood for. They offer you expert help, information, advice and support, free of charge when diagnosed with cancer. I was not really clear what she could do for me, unlike a lot of bread-winners to the household who have to stop work, I was very fortunate that I did not need financial help and felt she was there more as a sympathetic ear for someone who needed a crutch at such a distressing time. I thought it was very kind of her to come, I was not ungrateful, but I could not see what she could give me.

Meanwhile, I had to decide what was the best practical course of action for me. It was a horrific dilemma, as I had no medical training to help me, but in the end only I could make the decision. I opted for the chemotherapy and radiation.

Once I'd made my decision, Catherine Coyle, having received Pat Bradley's report, called me in immediately on the morning of Friday 20 September. It was now that I got to hear from her the problems I would face and how difficult it was going to be for me. Fortunately it turned out to be a case of 'we' and not 'I'. We were working together, and I soon came to realise that there was nobody better in the world to help me fight cancer than this frank and feisty, nearly 40-year-old Irish woman. She was dead straight with me, which I liked about her. Some people may not want to know the truth, but I did. I asked her if the treatment was going to be tough.

'Yes, very,' she said.

'What? Really tough?'

'Really, really tough!'

'Jesus Christ!' I replied. 'What are my chances?'

She answered that they were about 80 per cent. 'Can you give me ninety per cent?' I bargained. She was firm, and didn't try to be over-optimistic; she stressed that my chances were really good, and in an entirely different bracket from what they would have been if I had been a smoker or drinker. I then said: 'Well, if you save me I will kiss your arse' to which she blushed a little and laughed.

Catherine then asked me if I was on any tablets, so I explained about Chris Woollams and told her I was taking complementary stuff. Like most of the medical profession at the time, she did not really believe taking these types of tablets or going on specific diets helped with cancer, but she was open-minded enough to realise it was my body and I was going to do it regardless. All she asked was that I gave her a list of what I was taking at any given time, which I always did. In the weeks that followed there was only one herbal tablet she asked me not to take and explained why she thought it might interfere with what she was prescribing.

She wanted to give me two separate sessions of chemotherapy, the first starting that very day, so I was admitted into Cookridge Hospital for what was to be five days and nights of treatment. It started in Room 20 of the Rutherford Ward – I can still remember it now. I had a machine pumping horrible chemotherapy drugs, 5fu cisplatin it was called, hooked up to a vein in my arm 24 hours a day. It was not pleasant; Rachael likened it to mustard gas. What it does is kill all the fast-growing cells in your body, but unfortunately it does not discriminate between good cells and the cancer ones.

It was not immediate but eventually the drug destroyed all my saliva glands, and to this day they have unfortunately never come back. The chemotherapy also destroyed my taste buds, which did regenerate after about 12 months, and all my immune system, which took the best part of two years to be re-established.

While I was in hospital having this treatment, they also took me down to the 'Mould Room', as they called it, where they measured me up for the plastic mask I would need to wear during radiotherapy.

When I was discharged on 25 September, Catherine told me I had to see their dentist the next day to check all my teeth. It was the first I had heard about this and I wondered why I needed to go – I had cancer not cavities. I had been told I could be dead in three months, and so I was desperate for them to get on with the treatment, yet here they were sending me to the dentist.

Unbeknown to anybody else, 26 September was the date Rachael and I had made an appointment to visit the Register Office in Wakefield, in order to post the banns for our marriage. When I got home and told Rachael I had a dental appointment the next day, she just stared at me, and then I was reminded what we were supposed to be doing. There was so much going on I had forgotten all about it, and I said 'Oh fuck! I will cancel the dentist.' She said that we could reschedule the Register Office. In fact, when I rang to say we would have to cancel the appointment and gave them the reason why, the lady at the Register Office said she would come see us the next day at Woolley.

I wanted to get married before the treatment took hold, because if I died I did not want the tax man to get all my money, as I feel I have paid enough of that in my life. Rachael joked she was not too proud about the circumstances behind getting the ring, as long as it finally happened after all the years we had been together.

At the dental clinic I was told there was a problem with a

couple of my teeth, one in particular, a big molar on the right side. It turned out there was a gap between the tooth and the gum, and if it got infected with any bacteria it could be a serious problem once I started the radiation treatment. Osteoradionecrosis, as it is called, is a complication caused by radiation, because it impairs the blood supply to the bone in your gums and it dies. I was told removing my teeth would delay the radiotherapy for two to three weeks, because they would have to wait for the wounds to heal fully before commencing treatment.

I was angry. My teeth seemed healthy to me and I did not want any of them taken out. I thought that with cancer, time was of the essence, yet this had been going on since late August and here we were almost in October and I felt I still had not started the real treatment. I had only had some chemotherapy, but no laser treatment. They seemed to be taking forever and now they wanted to add in more delays while they took out some healthy teeth. I had cancer in my shoulder, neck and tongue, but I felt that if we had carried on like this I would end up having the most fantastic set of teeth in the morgue.

This was when I had a stroke of luck. As I had just come out of hospital after my first round of chemotherapy, the discharge liaison nurse from my GP's practice, Julie Maltman, came to see me early that evening, completely unannounced. She turned out to be a star. I did not know it at the time but our guardian angel had just walked into our lives.

I chatted to her about my teeth and she arranged for me to see another dentist in Heckmondwicke, Naresh Sharma, and he passed me on to his friend, Professor Monty Singh Duggal, who is head of child dental health in Leeds. He was brilliant and solved the problem. He confirmed there was one tooth which was a candidate for infection, as it did have a small gap where the gum had receded, so he gave me a syringe with corsodyl, an antiseptic and disinfectant, and told me to inject the hole every morning and evening. In fact I am still doing it today, 12 years later. The tooth has never been taken out and must be the healthiest, cleanest tooth in Yorkshire.

My life now consisted of an endless round of appointments. I had a 'mask fitting' on Tuesday 8 October at Cookridge, which took around three hours, it's not exactly like being fitted for a new suit. The next day saw me back again as they needed to look at my kidneys to check for damage caused by the chemotherapy, and that took approximately four hours, so along with the two-hour round trip in the car, another day was gone.

On the Thursday, we had arranged for a Chinese feng shui master to come up from London, with his delightful personal assistant, Jan Hassan, to visit our house in Woolley. I was open to anything, just trying to find things to help me stay alive. Rachael had dabbled in feng shui for a few years, so she persuaded me to have someone come and do a more personal reading for myself and our house. Rachael knew there are bad and good health 'houses', and felt we needed to have our home checked out.

My close friend at the time, Russell Homer, had used this particular feng shui master for his home in Jersey, so on his recommendation I got in touch with Master Li. We had previously furnished him with the exact time and dates of birth for Rachael, Emma and myself in order that he could prepare our individual readings before he came. He did not have a clue who I was, and in his broken English kept referring to me as

Mr Geoff because in his culture the first name is considered to be the polite way to address someone. His assistant Jan also had no idea about cricket or who I was or what I did.

Master Li explained that there is a health area in every house and we should have a small light on 24 hours a day in that area. He also advised us to put a water feature in the kitchen and he told me in what direction I had to sleep, with the back of my head facing south/south east for the rest of that Chinese year. Apparently you heal as you sleep, so it is important to know where to sleep. Rachael therefore moved me into a small single bedroom to accommodate this and also the chair in my 'snug' was moved in to a 'good' direction. He added that our health moves in ten-year cycles and mine had started when I was seven years old; he said it was written in my chart that I was going to have health problems from ages 57 to 67. Looking back that had been the case, but this was the most serious health problem by far.

He also said I would need to celebrate my 70th birthday with a big party, which we eventually did, but at the time I was not sure I would make that milestone. However, Rachael says that is when she knew, without doubt, I was going to survive this, and that is what kept her going in the 'terrible times'. Deep down she always had this certainty in her mind I would live.

On Monday 14 October, I made another journey to Cookridge for Catherine Coyle's review clinic and I weighed 85.4 kilos fully clothed. She told me to eat as much as I could because I would need to keep my strength up over the coming days, and she advised me to take regular exercise, so after my treatments in the morning I would go for a walk in the afternoon in Woolley Park.

The following day I returned for another mask fitting and then on Wednesday I had to attend a round of blood tests for the chemo treatment. Catherine Coyle told me she had booked me in for Monday 21 October to start my second round of chemo. I asked if I could go in the day after, as it was my birthday and I wanted to celebrate my 62nd because I thought it might be my last one. I did not tell her the real reason was that Rachael and I had scheduled our wedding for that day.

Catherine didn't want to delay things even by one day, however, as her tests had shown the first set of chemotherapy had been too strong and had destroyed too many white blood cells. Apparently there is no 'set dose' for this treatment, and the dosage is usually calculated on the basis of one's weight. She had originally wanted to give me five more days of chemotherapy, but could now give me only three days and she said this made it even more urgent to start the radiation treatment. So after the chemo gave my cancer its first powerful kick, I started laser treatment on Tuesday 22 October while still in hospital. It was the first of 35 daily sessions that ran for five days a week for seven very long weeks.

She explained that the effects would be particularly grim, because she wanted to give me the most aggressive dosage she thought I could stand, at strength 70, rather than the 50 or 60 which is more usual in the UK. Apparently she had done her training in France where this is the norm. Looking back I am glad I had her and that she was confident enough in her own skill to do this. It was bloody painful but I have no doubt it was one of the things that saved my life. Pat Bradley later said I was lucky to have her.

CHAPTER 4

THE FIGHTBACK BEGINS

At last I felt I was really beginning to move forward. We are constantly bombarded with advice telling us the importance of how catching cancer early can make the difference between life and death, but from the date of finding my tumour shaving in the mirror to having my first zap of radiation had taken almost ten weeks. Even if you take it from the date when it was confirmed as cancer, which was the night I went to the football at Old Trafford, then it had still taken seven weeks for the treatment to start. During that time I got increasingly angry and frustrated, because I wrongly felt it had been strung out for so long. I did not grasp that, by having the chemotherapy sessions, I had in fact already started my treatment. What was more, because of my name, I had been lucky that so many people had come into my life and helped speed things along.

It is during this period that cancer patients can become

irrational and feel life is unfair. The fear of dying grips your every waking hour, and yet the medical profession appears to be taking forever to start the treatment. While you want to rip out the tumour which is slowly snuffing out your life, they seem to be stalling. I now know that this is unfair, because the doctors have to pinpoint your treatment in order to make sure they do the right thing for you. But that was how I had felt in the few days leading up to my radiotherapy finally starting. Perhaps I would not have been so desperate to start had I known the pain that was in store for me.

During my chemotherapy treatment Chris Woollams had suggested I take something to counteract the side effects and to stop me vomiting. Thankfully it worked. He also warned me before I started my laser treatment that I needed to understand chemotherapy kills and destroys all the fast-growing cells in the body, and if my body was left to its own devices it could take up to two years for it to be fully restored. The immune system is so weakened by the treatment that you are vulnerable to viruses and illnesses during that period and for a long time afterwards.

With having only a small spleen I was even more susceptible to infections than normal, so had to take special precautions. Chris taught me the trick of putting Vaseline in my nostrils when I woke up in the morning. The hairs in your nose are the first line of defence for any airborne diseases and need to be moist and sticky to trap any germs. I did this whenever I went to hospital, as that is where the risk was at its greatest. A number of times I arrived at Cookridge and would see people there for treatment, and friends or family who had brought them to the hospital, sniffling. I was starting treatment just as we were heading in to winter, a season when colds are commonplace, so the risk was high. Even the receptionist was coughing and sneezing a lot one day, and I remember her saying she thought she had flu. If I had got anything it would have been very difficult to shake it off. The Vaseline must have really helped as I never once caught a cold, and I still keep up this treatment even now when travelling on a plane or any place where the air is circulating around. As a result, I've not had a cold to this day.

Chris sent me a tailor-made list of the herbal supplements he wanted me to take, as well as details of when to stop some and then start others. So I began taking different tablets to assist my body, and particularly my kidneys, to flush out all the dead cancer cells that he said would now be floating around my body after the chemotherapy.

In fact all around me I was receiving great support, and on the Friday after coming out of hospital, I rang my then boss at talkSPORT, Kelvin MacKenzie, to give him an update. He was fantastic. I know he can be over the top and divides opinion, but I loved working for him and knew I would have a job to go back to if my health returned, which took that particular worry out of my life.

For the next seven weeks our daily routine had to revolve around the trip to Cookridge and back. I had set my mind to recovery. This was what I needed to do: I counted the 35 sessions off like I would my runs when I was batting. I always had a gift when I was batting for knowing my own score. I counted every single one of them in each game I played and I did not need the scoreboard to know what I was on. When I played in matches with a primitive scoreboard or not very reliable scorers,

I would know if they had my score wrong. In one-day cricket I used to count my runs, how many an over we needed to win and whether we were above or below the asking rate. I went about it in exactly the same way when I had my treatment. I would count each and every one until we got to the halfway mark. I then felt I was heading for the finish line. I would fall asleep thinking: 'I have done five; it will be six tomorrow.' I focused on that to get me through.

My appointments at the start were at 9am, which was the first of the day, but in order to not be late I would have to set off by 7am. It was only about 20 miles away, but it necessitated going up the M1 and then through the centre of Leeds to get to the hospital, which was in the northern suburbs, so it wasn't straightforward. As time went on Rachael said this is silly and the radiologist agreed to move my session to just before lunch, which was more convenient in some ways, but more often than not I would have to wait a long time for my turn.

One day I went for my treatment and there was a young boy aged eight or nine with no hair left and he wouldn't or couldn't take any more. His mum, the nursing sister and head radiologist were all trying to persuade him to go in for another session of treatment, but he just sat on the chair in the waiting room with his head down, not talking. He'd just had enough. It was heartbreaking to see this small, scared child in such a state, but the shocking thing is it is a scene played out in every hospital, every day. As I looked on, the nursing sister, Sally Marshall, said to me: 'Don't miss any sessions, Geoffrey.' She then explained how my treatment had been worked out in advance and if I missed one they would have to recalculate everything. I said I wouldn't and I didn't.

I would have laser treatments Monday to Friday, with what Catherine Coyle called a session review every five days. The actual laser bit of the procedure would take only two or three minutes each time, but getting ready for it was another ball game. I would go into the treatment room and they would put my plastic mask in place. It looked so grotesque; I resembled the man in the iron mask. There were two holes for my eyes, two small ones for each nostril and a slit for my mouth so I could breathe. I would lie on the table and the mask would be bolted down with screws on either side of it.

In order for the technicians to know exactly where to blast my neck, Catherine had previously marked the mask with a cross where she wanted the laser to be aimed. It was imperative my head stayed absolutely still, because if the rays hit my spinal column I could have been paralysed from the neck down. Meanwhile, the laser would move on its own accord as programmed, to various angles starting on the good side of my face, the right side, before moving to the left where the tumour was.

In the early days of this treatment, I drove myself to the hospital and could not see any marks on my neck. I was eating normally, if you could say my new food 'regime' was normal, and taking a daily walk in the park. It didn't seem as bad as I had been led to expect. By the time I had my first session review after five days, I was starting to get a dry mouth, even though I was producing more mucus than normal as a side effect of the chemotherapy.

It was on one of my weekend breaks from chemotherapy, Sunday 10 November, that Rachael drove me to Leicestershire to see Dr Patrick Kingsley, a specialist in holistic medicine that Chris Woollams had suggested I go see. Patrick asked me to fill in a questionnaire about my life and health, which helped him form answers to the question that had been bothering me from day one, namely: why did I get this cancer? From the answers I gave him, he came up with five possible reasons: dairy intolerance, zinc from my fillings, radiation exposure from flying, inoculations and stress.

It was the first time I had been told I had an intolerance to dairy products. He deduced this from the fact that whenever I had contracted a cold it would always move to my chest and I would then need antibiotics to clear it up. But the most telling factor for him was that throughout my teens I had lots of problems with catarrh and sore throats, leading to my tonsils being removed at the age of 22. This is a relatively late age for that kind of operation and coincidentally my daughter Emma had to have hers removed around the same age, too.

In terms of the fillings, he said that each time I brushed my teeth, in my case two or three times a day, a bit of zinc would go down my throat from my metal fillings. He believed the amount of air travel during my cricket and commentary career put me at risk of accumulated exposure to the radiation we are subjected to on airplanes. People do not realise how much radiation there is in the cabin of an aeroplane. During my life I'd been administered lots of inoculations, in the belief I did not have a spleen and thus lacked natural defences to infections. Research has shown there was a possible link between cancer and hepatitis injections.

Stress was the final suggestion he had. He knew who I was and what I did and pointed out that I had spent all my life as a professional sportsman in a 'goldfish bowl' in front of the media and public. He thought the final straw might have been going through the 'French farce', as the press dubbed it, which was my court case. This came on top of Chris Woollams's theory I had been carrying parasites picked up during my time in the subcontinent, which is why he had previously recommended I take the ParaFree drug and probiotics. Finally, I was starting to find some clarity as to why I had contracted this horrible disease, but now the most important thing was to concentrate on the cure.

Before we left, he took lots of blood samples to send away and said I would need copious amounts of vitamins and supplements to combat what my body was going through. He recommended intravenous injections as being the quickest way to do this and suggested I get in touch with Dr Damian Downing, a nutritionist based in York. This was something we had never heard of before, but now once a week Rachael would drop me off, giving her time to escape and do the food shopping, while I would have a drip put in my arm and instantly fall asleep for an hour. I have since learnt that nowadays celebrities are apparently having these intravenous sessions before their gigs or heavy nights partying. For me the reason was very different.

On 14 November, Catherine Coyle made an appointment for me at the hospital with Hayley, her nutritionist, who explained that they would need to fit a tube to feed me when the pain from the burns in my mouth and throat became too much to bear. I was strongly against this suggestion and looking back I think I saw it as a sign of weakness and was determined to stay away from it as long as I could, even though eating food was beginning to become more difficult.

We tried to keep life at home as normal as possible, and

Rachael insisted from very early on that no one was going to die and there would be no pussyfooting around me in the house by anyone. She decided for all our sakes that it was important, when we could, to keep some humour and laughter in our lives. She used to say to me when I was being un-cooperative or grumpy: 'Stop it! You are just ill, you are not dying!'

I remember that on the weekend of 16 November we took Emma to see the newly released Harry Potter film at the local cinema, because she and I both loved the films and it was important that our daughter had as much normality in her life as possible. It was fortunate that she was at boarding school and not there all the time, so Emma did not see me distressed and in difficulty every day.

By week four the pain had started to increase and the burns on my skin really hurt; it was agony. My brother Tony or the local taxi driver, Mick Hough, had been taking me to my daily appointments for some time, but now I needed Rachael's help. As the radiation built up, I developed terrible raw burns and they had to be covered up in case of infection. First to go was the skin on my collar bones, then my neck and eventually the skin on my left cheek. We were given some pale pink sponge-like pads that needed taping over the open wounds. When it was removed, if any of the tape even touched what looked like good skin, it would rip it off and cause agony.

Rachael devised various shapes in order to fit the afflicted areas and eventually I had pads all round my neck, which she said made me look as if I was wearing a vicar's dog collar. Before the radiation started they would take the burn pads off and that was the worst moment of all; the pain as the cold air hit the burns was enough to make me want to scream. It would last only for a few seconds, until they put a protective cling film over the oozing wounds, so the pus did not get on the mask during treatment, but of course the pain would start over again when they removed everything.

While I was having my sessions every day, Rachael would find a vacant nurses' room nearby and get some fresh burn pads ready, she would usher me in and cover up the skin as hastily as possible. The nurses would not always be free immediately I came out of the treatment room, as they were often busy with other patients, so they did not mind Rachael doing it instead, as it ensured I did not have to lie there in agony waiting.

Although the skin was now badly burnt, every session made it worse but I had to keep going for more treatment on red raw skin. It needed all my mental strength to get up in the morning, go to the hospital and have more radiation. Every brain cell is screaming at you not to go, but you have to fight the temptation to give up and stay at home.

I was still travelling to York for my vitamin treatments, even though by now I needed Rachael's help just to get me dressed in the mornings. Unfortunately, I was no longer getting any effect from my pain-relief tablets, so eating was becoming tough. Rachael had been mashing up all my food into a puree, so it was like eating baby food, and she had even been crushing my tablets into powder and putting that in the food so I could swallow them. But because the pain relief was not working anymore, I was finding it increasingly difficult to swallow anything.

Our guardian angel, nurse Julie Maltman, came to the rescue. She brought me some morphine pain patches to put on my arm, which slowly infused into my body and helped stop the pain. When I first started using them, I began with one patch at strength 25 and it lasted for 72 hours. However, the more treatment I had, the worse the pain; I had to increase the number of patches, so I ended up with three, the maximum dosage allowed.

As my treatment continued, my energy levels started to deplete so I spent most of my time at home just lying in my reclining chair. I was so tired and weak when I came back from the hospital I did not even want to get up and go to the toilet. I would watch television in the afternoons, something I had never done in my life, but as I was quite doped up I would fall asleep, so I might see the beginning of a programme, but very rarely stayed awake to the end.

Ironically, I found that my favourite programme was *Ready Steady Cook*, in which two contestants, one wearing a red tomato apron and the other a green pepper, competed against each other, with the studio audience voting as to who had cooked the better dish. It was weird because I could no longer eat, had no appetite or even any taste buds left and I had never been interested or watched anything remotely like this. Rachael would have to watch it wherever she was in the house, because if I missed the ending I had to know who had won.

Despite how I was feeling, every morning when I got up I would force myself to go for a walk because at that time I would be at my freshest. No matter how cold it was, I would still go out, wrapped up in an enormous overcoat and scarf. By this time I had stopped walking into the village, as Rachael was concerned I might collapse. I worked out if I walked 20 laps around our tennis court it was close enough to a mile and she would keep checking I was okay from the house, while she was doing the chores.

By Wednesday 4 December I was losing weight alarmingly, and had shed ten pounds in one week. Rachael had shopped to buy me some trousers that did not fall off me and also bought some thick woollen cardigans, as I had no proper winter clothes. It was the first whole winter I had spent in England for nearly 40 years, and I hate the cold. The burn blisters in my mouth were agonising; we have thousands of nerve endings in our gums and on our tongue, and I had huge blisters everywhere in my mouth. They were raging sores that even the slightest touch would aggravate, so eating food was impossible. It was a tough time and I was getting seriously ill.

I was now sleeping all the time because of the morphine, not eating and even struggling to drink. In fact water was the hardest thing to swallow, even more than pureed food. It was obvious I could not go on much longer like this, but I still had four of my 35 sessions of radiation treatments to go. It is not just what the cancer does to you, it is the treatment. I kept resisting having the feeding tube inserted, because I somehow thought it would indicate I had given up and the disease had defeated me.

I had been going to my weekly review sessions and trying to fool them when they weighed me by stuffing my cardigan pockets with heavy coins and putting a handkerchief on top to stop them clinking together and alerting them to what I really weighed. I knew that once I fell to a certain weight, they would insist on putting what I thought was this horrible tube up my nose, so I did my best to delay it as long as I could. I feared it because it was the unknown and also the kind of thing worn by really sick people. Of course I was sick, but I did not want to admit I had fallen to such a low ebb.

Looking back now, I realise my subterfuge was only making matters worse. In the end they saw through it and, as Rachael says, I looked so god-awful anyway. After weighing me that day, Sally Marshall went off to speak to Catherine Coyle, who came straight away and said: 'I want you in hospital now!'

I tried to bluff her and said I would need to go home to get some clothes, but she was having none of it. My weight was dangerously low and I was having the tube fitted there and then whether I liked it or not. There are two options when you are having a tube fitted: either you can have one straight into your stomach through an opening, but Chris Woollams had advised me against that due to the possibility of infection, so I opted for the tube through my nose. This involved a nurse inserting it up my nose and telling me to swallow so it could be pushed down in to my stomach. It was not a very pleasant experience but actually, like most things in life, the fear and dread of it happening was actually worse than the event itself. I had to just accept the fact I was now going to be fed by a machine.

It was hardly an inconspicuous piece of kit, and I was not going to be able to hide it from public view. For a start the tube was yellow, not skin-coloured, and taped to my nose where it came out, to keep it secure. It went across my cheek, rested on top and behind my ear then dangled down to my chest. On the end of the tube was a tap or port, as it was called, and through this my medicines and water would be inserted with a syringe. When it came to feeding me, each time a new sterile tube would need fixing to the port, which then ran to a bag of liquid feed and that was hooked up to a machine that pumped it into me. I needed two and a half bags a day, which would take about eight hours.

The following day when Rachael returned to hospital, the nurses showed her how to use the feeding tube. They said I would not be able to go home until they were satisfied she knew how to deal with it. The first step was to make sure it was still going down into my stomach. They explained that at no time should I ever be allowed to lie completely flat, even through the night, in case I coughed it up into my lungs, which could have lethal consequences should liquid then be poured down it. Using a syringe attached to the port, Rachael would draw some liquid and test it for its pH value on a piece of litmus paper. The tube would then need rinsing out with a clean syringe full of sterile water, before the feeding process could begin.

A few weeks previously, knowing the tube was inevitable at some stage, Rachael had asked the dieticians at Cookridge what was in the bags of feed they would be giving me. When they told her it was lots of goodness mostly consisting of milk and sugar she had pointed out that I was intolerant to dairy and that cancer loves sugar. The nutritionist said there was no alternative, but fortunately Rachael had her wits about her and knew there was a soya feed that Chris Woollams had told her about. Hayley had never heard of it and was sceptical but promised she would look into it. About three days later, she phoned Rachael saying she had tracked down the soya feed and ordered a case of 12 bottles for a start and would keep it ready for me when I needed it. She was a lovely lady and so helpful.

In time we became accustomed to using the machine and found when at home the best way to encourage the fastest flow would be for me to lie in my reclining armchair in the snug with the pump propped up high on an antique plant stand. It was quite a sight, and apart from anything else Rachael would joke that my nose, all squished up with tape holding the tube in place, made me look like Michael Jackson. I did not care; I was relieved because it meant an end to the constant fear of eating or drinking and the dread of having the tube fitted was over.

Unfortunately, at the same time the tube was fitted the hospital staff were given orders to take me off the morphine patches because they were too expensive. It was a bitter blow, as it meant I had to take the medicine through the tube and, unlike before, there were now periods when I had to wait for it to kick in.

On my third day in hospital, Rachael had to learn how to administer the liquid morphine down the tube, and what a palaver it was. She had to check the tube was in my stomach, wash it out, put the red medicine in, wash it out again and then hook it up to a feeding bag. They even wanted me to learn how to do it as well, but there was no chance I could manage it. The new drug routine had started on 4 December, when I was given two millilitres of pure morphine to control the pain every six hours, and if the pain got worse I could have an extra 20 millilitres of a diluted morphine if I requested it. It seemed a fairly straightforward system.

As I only had one session of radiation left, on Monday 9 December, they decided I might as well stay in hospital over the weekend so the nurses could keep an eye on me. However, I had already made plans for the Saturday night and the Sunday morning, so it was agreed I could be 'sprung' out of hospital for these, as long as I returned.

Months before I knew I had cancer, I had booked for the three of us to go to the Grand Theatre in Leeds to see *The Nutcracker*. I enjoy the classical ballets and Emma, like most young teenage girls, loved dancing and she had never seen a live ballet performance. Rachael went home on the Friday night leaving me with strict instructions to be dressed when she arrived back with Emma the next afternoon, before we went out that evening. She was concerned that Emma, not having seen me for a couple of weeks, would be distressed enough at my appearance dressed, never mind how I looked undressed. By now, having lost 50 pounds (about 22 kilos), I resembled a wizened old man of 90, while naked I looked like I had just come out of a concentration camp.

When they arrived in the ward, Rachael was met by the nursing sister who explained that unfortunately that afternoon I had gone to sleep flat on my bed and had coughed the tube out. Apparently, I had agreed to wait for her coming to discuss if it should be put back in before we went to the ballet. Rachael was not best pleased after all the instructions she'd had the day before about ensuring she did not let me lie flat, but suggested it would probably be best to leave the tube out until I returned from the theatre. She knew I could still be recognised in the audience when we went out, and it would be kinder not to have people staring at me with a yellow tube across my face.

I cannot remember them walking into my room, and I am told it was not a pretty sight with me lying on the bed naked and then jumping up in an agitated state trying to get dressed. Rachael says Emma was obviously taken aback, but then just hugged me and helped me to dress.

I really do not recall much at all, but I liked the show and

Emma tells me I was grinning like a Cheshire cat at people. I tried to drink some water from a straw during the interval but struggled with that. When we left the theatre and went back to the car, Emma says I walked straight into a lamp-post with my shoulder and bounced off it and said: 'Sorry, I apologise.' Emma whispered to her mum: 'Dad is talking to the lamp-post.'

Rachael got the impression that if she had said 'jump off that cliff', I would have said 'yes, dear'. As she said later, this would have been most un-Geoffrey like! When we arrived back at the hospital, Rachael parked right outside the entrance to my wing and put me in the lift, which I had been in many times before. I needed to get out at the second floor, and as the corridor had all-glass windows, they could watch from the car to make sure I walked into the ward. I had to turn left into my ward, while the main hospital, which was pretty much in darkness with it being a Saturday night, was to my right. What did I do? I turned right and disappeared out of their sight. Emma then rushed up the stairs to find me and take me back to my ward and handed me over to the nurses.

The following morning Rachael was at home with Emma fast asleep in our bed, when the phone rang next to it. As she remembers it, she heard my croaky voice at the other end say: 'What time is it?'

'It's eight thirty.'

'In the morning or at night?'

'In the morning. Why didn't you ask the nurses?'

'Why? Where am I?' I replied.

'You're in hospital, love. In Cookridge.'

'Thank fuck for that. I thought the IRA had got me.'

All I remember of our conversation was waking up in a panic, lying in bed gripped with fear in a sparse, enclosed room with a very small window. I had a tube up my nose and there was a machine on the bedside table. It was dark in there and I was scared to get up. I was staring at the door frightened of what was behind it. I waited for a little while not knowing what to do, then I saw my mobile phone and knowing my home number off by heart managed to ring Rachael.

Because of my behaviour the night before and now this, she knew immediately something was not right and took action. She had to drop Emma back at boarding school that morning for a school trip, so rang Mick Hough, who had been driving me around in the early days of my treatment, and asked him to go and pick me up immediately. She told him not to take any non-sense or arguments from the nurses, and to get me to sign any forms I needed to discharge myself. I was not to walk down the stairs, but to use the lift and he was to keep hold of me at all times. She said he was to bring everything with me, because the duvet, pillows and towels were mine, and he was to tell the nurses I was not coming back. Rachael was not messing around. He did exactly as she had said, and the nurses gave Mick my pain medication, in two separate bottles, to bring home with me.

Weeks before, I had arranged a meeting with my local councillor, Norman Hazell, for that day, so Rachael was due to come and get me from hospital anyway. When Mick got me home, he stayed until the councillor came to drive us to Fitzwilliam, the village where I grew up.

For months I had been lobbying the local authorities to do something to help Fitzwilliam, which had fallen into dereliction since the closure of the mine in the late 1980s. My brother

Tony, a lovely man who helped me no end during my cancer treatment, still lived in the area and his terraced house was two streets from where we grew up with my parents, at 45 Milton Terrace. Tony had been coming to help tend my garden at Woolley and for some time had been telling us horror stories about youths setting fire to the roofs of the empty houses next door to him, stealing lead, downpipes, guttering and using unoccupied houses as drug dens.

He had taken me back to Milton Terrace to see how it had become, and it was a mess. The house we had lived in as kids had been demolished, and was now just a pile of rubble and bricks. The rows of houses still standing were in an awful state, and in my brother's street there were about eight houses, including his, that were still in a good condition and nicely kept, but the rest had either broken or boarded-up windows. If you had seen someone in a 4×4 car, wearing dark glasses with a big AK47 poking out the window, you would have thought you were in Beirut. It was heartbreaking to see the area I loved as a child end up in this state.

Tony had bought his house with his redundancy money when Kinsley Drift mine closed in 1986, but now he was stuck with it. He could not sell up and move away because nobody wanted to buy houses in that area. It was the same for his neighbours; these decent people were living in an awful area and they had no escape route. It was disgraceful and I had pushed for months to organise this meeting at my brother's house with Norman, Peter Loosemore, the Wakefield Council minister in charge of housing regeneration, and Kevin Dodd, the chief housing officer for that area.

The only day they could make was that Sunday so I had to

go regardless of the state I was in. I must have looked almost as run down as the houses, with a feeding tube in my nose, very gaunt and hunched over, but I was determined to make sure these men would take action. After a short chat, I took them round the estate and explained that we needed the council to compulsorily purchase, for a reasonable amount, the houses of the people who were stuck there. The council had already done this for other streets and then knocked the houses down, but Marlene, Tony's wife, had been told it could be a few more years before it would be their turn.

At the end of the tour, I invited the three men to return the following Sunday. I said to them: 'I would like you to bring your wives and I'm going to ask them one question: "Would you like to live here with your children?" One simple question, because I know what the answer will be. If the answer is "no", then why should you expect other citizens to live here?'

I left them to think on that while I went home. Some months later, I was delighted when the council came through for Tony and Marlene with an offer they could accept, and with my help they bought a lovely bungalow nearer to their daughter.

By the time I returned to Woolley, Rachael was back at home and I was due my morphine before she hooked me up to my feeding machine. After a while, she could sense something was not right again; I was hyperactive and could not keep still, so she rang Julie Maltman for advice and, although it was a Sunday, she came straight over. She was puzzled and could not work out why I was behaving so strangely and left saying she would be back the next day. But about ten minutes later, on her way home, she rang from her car and asked Rachael to say what was on the labels of the two bottles of morphine.

Rachael read out the contents and the dosage on each bottle. A light went on in Julie's head: she realised the hospital had mixed up the two dosages. Instead of giving me 2 millilitres of pure morphine and 20 of diluted morphine, they had been doing it the other way around. For four days I had been getting 20 millilitres of pure morphine every four-to-six hours and tripping on one of the most powerful drugs known to man. It all started to make sense: grinning through the ballet, talking to the lamp-post, getting lost in the hospital and fearing I had been kidnapped by the IRA. I had been hallucinating on a morphine high. Julie said I was lucky, for if my system had not already been accustomed to the drug, taking 20 millilitres of pure morphine could have killed me. She told Rachael to flush me out with as much water as possible and to stop the liquid morphine.

When I went to the hospital the following day for my last laser treatment, the nursing sister asked me why I had left hospital the previous day. Rachael relayed the whole story and the cock-up with the medicines. I saw Catherine Coyle two days later at her weekly clinic and while reading my notes she just glanced up at Rachael and said: 'Oh I see you are back on the pain patches, well that's fine.' They both looked at each other and nothing more was said. We could have taken it further with the hospital, but I was alive, thanks to Rachael's intuition and Julie's knowledge.

I was told after the laser treatment finished that the radiation would still be in my body for two to three weeks, a bit like a microwave I would still be 'cooking', and as it turned out I was in real difficulty for the rest of December.

When Emma came home for her leave-out weekends, she was always full of energy and her mum made sure she too was looked after. She was a teenager and needed attention from her mum, but Rachael had taught her how to flush the tube and change my feeding bottle to keep her involved in my recovery. Rachael could not leave me on my own, because I was unable to work the feeding machine if anything went wrong, so when Emma came home for the Christmas holiday it was a huge help to her mum and having my 'little nurse' around cheered me also. We had to have as much normality as possible in the house, and Emma taking over the feeding just became another part of our routine.

During this period, Rachael never tiptoed around me, she would tell me off if I was un-cooperative or grumpy, and she became my companion and carer instead of my lover. Her role had completely changed. When visitors came to see me, I would say: 'Have you met my new jailer?' Even though I was now a lot sicker, it was still important to have jokes and laughter in the house to keep everyone's spirits up. Rachael would joke I had saved a fortune having a chemical peel on my cheeks, free of charge by the NHS.

We had a range of people who came to see me, or who kept in touch by phone. Martin Edwards, the president of Manchester United, popped in for coffee one day, while Sally Anne Hodson would often call with messages from her brother Tony Greig. Lots of cricketing friends like Darren Gough, Arnie Sidebottom and Barry Wood either stopped by or called. In fact, Barry relieved me of some of my best red wine on a few occasions. Every other Sunday morning throughout my illness, Fred Trueman rang when he got home from church and would ask Rachael how I was doing. Sometimes I was well enough to talk and if not she would give him an update.

I can remember one time during that period when he was beside himself. He kept saying: 'Have you seen what that pillock Roy Hattersley has written in the Sunday paper? He's been asked to pick his all-time greatest Yorkshire side and he's left you out. Can you believe it? And he's picked two left-arm spinners [Wilfred Rhodes and Hedley Verity] – just shows how much he knows about cricket.'

On Christmas Day, I sat at the table in our conservatory for lunch with Rachael, Emma, Rachael's parents, her brother Mick and his wife Glenda. For their sake I tried to eat some mashed-up food, but really could not manage it. I was in such a mess because my burns were at their fiercest and I had ulcers on the side of my tongue which had grown to the size of the nail on your little finger. My tongue was swollen and grotesque, and if I caught the ulcers on my teeth the pain was excruciating. I had to go back and lie in my chair. When Rachael came in from Christmas lunch, she could tell I was in a bad way. I had a handkerchief coming out of my closed mouth, covering my tongue trying to stop it from catching on my teeth.

Seeing that, she asked: 'You do not have to say anything, but is that to protect your tongue touching your teeth?' All I could do was nod. By this time I had three 25-strength morphine patches on my arm, but the pain was still getting through. Rachael had never sent for my GP, Dr Tony Sweeney, before but I was so distressed she called him and he came out on Christmas Day, took one look and administered a morphine injection straightaway. Alan Knott had phoned me from Cyprus on Christmas Eve and I'd managed a quick chat with him, but when Ali Bacher and Asif Iqbal among others telephoned the next day, Rachael had to tell them I was not well enough to talk.

Over Christmas and New Year the office of Dr Downing, the man I went to for vitamin injections, was closed but a doctor I had met a few years before, David Fieldhouse, came to help. He drove all the way from his house near the Dales to my home on 28 December just to give me this vitamin infusion. I was touched by his kindness.

Chris Woollams had said I needed to have acupuncture as soon as my laser treatment was over, because it would help my immune system get up and running, which in turn would help my energy levels. So I started going to see a specialist in Chesterfield called Robin Crowley who is a master at acupuncture. It meant that I was now having two long car trips every week: one to see Robin and another for my vitamin infusion.

The feeding tube remained long after the radiation therapy finished while my mouth and tongue healed, and it became normal to take the pump with me everywhere. Because it took eight hours for the food to be dripped into my stomach, and you are not allowed to feed while asleep at night, I could not afford to lose half the day not feeding when being driven to York or Chesterfield. Fortunately, the pump could run off a battery so Rachael would sit it on the middle console between the two of us, I would recline my seat as far back as possible to help gravity ease the flow of liquid down the tube. The pump became my constant companion – I even had to take it to the toilet with me. Every week I would also go to Catherine Coyle's clinic, and on Monday 13 January she took the tube out to see if I could manage to eat without it. I was pleased at this sign of progress, but it proved to be a false dawn.

There were other signs that I was getting better. My neck was healing, the dressings had gone and I was starting to look healthier and was down to having only one morphine patch on my arm. I was even able to get out of the house a bit more, and on 17 January I attended a function at the Town Hall in Leeds. I continued to try other therapies that might help. I went to a place in Upton, West Yorkshire, to try reiki, a Japanese therapy which believes in the power of hand healing on the body, but it did not do it for me, and I preferred to stick with the acupuncture.

My television employers, ESPN, had stayed in constant touch and were a great support throughout the whole thing, passing on the many letters and faxes of goodwill they had received from the public in India. They were one of the best companies I have ever worked for. As soon as I had been diagnosed with cancer, I had ceased working but they honoured my contract all the way through my illness. Every month I expected them to stop, but they never mentioned it and just continued to pay a not inconsiderable sum of money into my bank account. I shall always be very grateful for their support and as soon as I was feeling a bit better, Rachael encouraged me to get in touch with them and I did a live interview on the telephone on Tuesday 21 January. It was my first step back into what resembled work.

Three days later, I went to Fitzwilliam to open a nursing home for the elderly but that day I overdid it a bit, spending a long time on my feet, talking to people. When Julie called that night for her routine visit, she suggested I increase the morphine patches back to two because I was in a lot of pain. I was trying to move on with my life and rediscover some normality, but the pain in my throat would come flooding back, reminding me not to get carried away.

Saturday 1 February was the start of the Chinese New Year and in 2003 it was the year of the goat. The previous year I had slept with the back of my head facing south-east, but in the year of the goat I now had to have it facing north-east. The best direction every year is different for each individual, and is still something I practise today. Moving bedrooms felt like a new start, as if we were leaving the bad year behind, but even though we were trying to be normal by going out a bit, I was still not very strong. I remained little more than skin and bone, having lost all that weight and gaining energy was a slow process.

With the feeding tube gone, I was struggling to eat and because I had lost all my saliva glands and taste buds it became doubly difficult to get any food down. Rachael was spending ages in the kitchen, cooking fresh organic food for me, which she would then blend or mash up, to make it softer and easier to swallow. Despite doing all that, she was then still having to cajole or force me to get it down.

Unsurprisingly, sometimes she would get mad and frustrated with me, and I would get very cross at her because she did not seem to realise how difficult or painful it was. She said she was being cruel to be kind; I said she was just being cruel and that was her nature. I did not really mean it, of course; I was just feeling terrible and knew she was fighting hard to do her best for me. She also kept on giving me brown rice, which Stacey Darrell had recommended, but I hated the stuff. I warned her that when I was better, if she ever served up brown rice again she could shove it up where the monkey keeps his nuts! It may be good for you, but I vowed that as soon as I was well, every packet of the horrible stuff would go in the bin.

Eventually, on 12 February, Catherine decided I would need the feeding tube inserted again because for four weeks and three days I had not progressed. Cancer recovery is not a straight line, it has bends and ups and downs. My throat was getting better, then it would get worse, the pain would subside and I would start to get back to normality only for it to return again. It tested my mental strength to accept every setback. I tried to get off the morphine so my body would not become dependent on the drug, but it was difficult as the pain had not gone away. Now, although I had the tube back in, I was still supposed to be trying to get used to swallowing and eating food, alongside the liquid feed. I was trying, but as Rachael says I was very trying for her!

On 14 February, Emma thought I should take Mummy and her out for a meal to celebrate Valentine's Day. We went to one of our favourite restaurants, the Three Acres, and it was a lovely evening. There was nothing on the menu I felt I could get down, so they were marvellous and made me scrambled eggs which I did eat, but when I got home I had to put a patch on to dull the pain. I was so desperate to know when things were going to get better I even turned to astrology. I was just searching for anything to give me hope, to know how long it would be before I was back to normal. Fortunately, I had something to take my mind off my cancer.

CHAPTER 5

REMISSION
AND RENEWAL

The previous year we'd had two abortive attempts to arrange a date for our wedding day, but my cancer treatments had overtaken them and so, after the second time, when on my birthday I was called in to start my second chemotherapy session, Rachael had said: 'Right I am not marrying you until you are well.'

I was not exactly 'well' but my treatments had finished, so we decided it was now time and we set the date for 26 February. We had been through so much and just wanted a quiet day with our family and close personal friends. The last thing we wanted was the press finding out and taking pictures, turning it into a media scrum.

The registrar at Wakefield Register Office helped us to keep it all quiet. The banns had already been posted five months previously on 27 September, before the ravages of the disease had taken its toll on me. Norma Stroud had come to the house to discuss arrangements for us to fill in the forms. Instead of us going to see her and risk the chance of being spotted, and someone guessing what we were up to at the register office, Norma suggested we did not provide our full address and leave out the first line, 'Pear Tree Farm', and just put '2 Water Lane, Woolley'. She explained the wedding banns would be displayed on the noticeboard at the register office, and when the press came in they would merely glance at it on their way upstairs to the deaths department to see who had died. Apparently they usually just looked at the addresses and not the names, because the only people they were interested in seeing getting married were prisoners in Wakefield jail. Norma was right and we were lucky that not one press man had clocked it at that time.

I was not well enough to traipse around a load of jewellery shops, and again we did not want to risk anyone recognising me buying a wedding ring, so Emma went with her mum to choose one. However, I still wanted a say, so told Emma she had my vote as well as her own, because she is very like me and I trusted her to pick something I would approve of. This meant she had two votes so could over-rule her mum, which tickled her pink.

We invited only about two dozen guests, telling them not to be late arriving at our house and to get all dressed up for a lunch to celebrate my recovery. The word 'wedding' was not mentioned in the invitation, but one or two of the females had guessed. Unfortunately my brother Tony and his wife Marlene had already booked to go on holiday so they could not be there.

Everyone arrived at 11.30 and they were then requested to drive down to the register office in Wakefield. Richard Knaggs, my best man, and Emma, the only bridesmaid, knew our secret. The registrar, Mr Hodgson, and his staff were brilliant and kept it all confidential. I was lucky that the press did not have a clue, and the news only came out a few days later, when the marriage had been registered at Somerset House in London.

The news of our wedding was all over the dailies but they had no real details or any pictures, so we had reporters camped at the bottom of our drive for a few days, but to no avail. Then my youngest brother, Peter, started opening his mouth. Again. Although I had no proof, I was pretty sure he had taken money from newspapers during my playing career for information about me, usually when they wanted to get at me for something, and as a result I had blocked him out of my life.

Even when my daughter Emma was born in 1988, Peter had been the only member of my family to speak to the press. Although, true to form, what he told them was a load of drivel, because we'd had no contact for years. When I was starting to recover from the cancer treatment, Tony, our middle brother, who still saw Peter, told me: 'Our Pete would like to come to Woolley and see you.' My first thought was no but Rachael had been working on me, and although I hadn't said anything to anyone I was coming round to it. So, a few days after our wedding, I was really annoyed to see Peter spouting that 'the family knew nothing about it' and 'I wasn't invited and my brother Tony didn't go'. It was as if he was privy to my life, and I was really angry. Unsurprisingly, after that the reconciliation never took place.

For the wedding ceremony, I surprised Rachael and pulled my feeding tube out, but I knew I would need to go back to the hospital the following day to have it put back in. Catherine Coyle was concerned when I turned up without it, but forgave me when I told her the reason why I had taken it out. She congratulated us both and said if the next month went well I would be strong enough to fly long haul if we wanted to go on holiday.

At the time, the World Cup was on in South Africa and ESPN had asked me if I would like to do a little work for them. All I had to do was watch the matches on the television and then they would call me afterwards for a quick interview. It gave me something to concentrate on, other than being unwell and trying to recover.

The other thing that people forget is that, just because you have got cancer, your other illnesses or problems do not disappear. On Thursday 20 March I went to Leeds Nuffield Hospital for an injection in the facet joint of my back. I had first injured it in 1968, playing for England in a Test match against Australia at Edgbaston, and it nearly finished my career. As a result of all this sitting and lying down over the previous few weeks, it was playing up and giving me some discomfort.

Four days later, I was back at Cookridge Hospital to see Catherine Coyle and, nearly 16 weeks after it had first been inserted, she said the tube could finally be removed. For a couple of weeks, I had been slowly reintroducing semi-solid food alongside the feeding tube, but this felt like a significant step in my recovery. Having all of my taste buds destroyed was both good and bad news. Rachael would prepare food I used to like the taste of, with a sauce or gravy to help me swallow, reasoning that if I knew I liked it in the past, it might be easier to eat it. However, unbeknown to me, in order to help me gain weight, she would add loads of natural fruit sugar to my portion and not just in desserts but savoury food, too.

As I started to eat more normally again, I was once more fighting with Rachael over my eating. I would move the food around on my plate, chop it up and play with it or have a nibble, even though there was nothing to chew. Rachael would watch me for a while and then eventually lose patience and say: 'For God's sake, put it in your mouth and swallow. You're acting like a young anorexic girl.' It was as though I had lost the art of eating, I was just not used to it and had to relearn how to deal with food.

Julie Maltman was a great support to both of us. Right from the beginning, she had got into a routine of calling on her way home most nights, having finished work for the day. Julie would have a drink with Rachael and catch up, while at the same time she would be studying me. She would sit at the table with us and try to distract me into eating my dinner. The best at that, though, was Emma. When she was at home she would make me laugh and spoon feed me saying: 'Now that's the way to do it, Daddy.' She thought it was hilarious that even carrots and chicken tasted of sugar and I did not know, but her mother had sworn her to secrecy.

Although I was not gaining much weight, and always had the cancer shadowing my every move, I was thankfully now emerging back into real life. The first step was our family holiday to South Africa, which had been a target motivating me through some of the dark moments of the previous weeks.

On 27 March my two girls and I flew to Johannesburg and then had a car drive us to Pecanwood Golf Estate, near the

Hartbeespoort Dam where my friend Ricky Roberts, who caddied for Ernie Els, lent us his house. We stayed there for a lovely week and I even began hitting golf balls again on the range, but I did not have the strength to play a proper round, even with the use of a buggy. There was a private plunge pool at the front of his home, overlooking the lake and all three of us would go in to relax in the evening.

One night, without my knowledge, Rachael took a photograph of me from behind, towelling down naked. For the second and third week of our vacation, we had arranged to meet up at the Sun City resort, about an hour's drive away, with Richard Knaggs, his wife Allison and my two young godchildren, Richard Jnr and Tara. Once there, Rachael got the photograph printed and gave it to me over dinner. It was a huge shock. She had done it deliberately to show me what I looked like. I was that thin I resembled one of those skeletons you see in the doctor's office, but with some skin still hanging off it. Rachael said she was sick of me 'pussyfooting around' with my food and wanted to jolt me into realising I had to eat properly.

The mouth blisters were all healed but eating normally was still tricky. My taste buds and saliva glands had been destroyed by the treatment and my appetite was a long way from returning to normal. I was managing small mouthfuls but could not cope with big meals. I do not like using this analogy, but to be blunt I looked like someone who had just come out of a concentration camp. I was a shrivelled old man and seeing that picture was a turning point for me. I decided my next goal was to do something about putting the weight back on. I kept that photograph in my wallet for quite a long time and would look at it if ever I needed encouragement to eat.

It was on this holiday that we also started making plans for the future, even though I didn't know at this stage if I had a future. I had always talked about having a house in South Africa, having fallen in love with the country on my first England tour in 1964. A close friend of mine, a Leeds lad actually, had been the golf professional at Stellenbosch in the Western Cape for a lot of years and he had told me about a new Jack Nicklaus-designed golf course being built near Paarl, with plots for houses on it.

Graham Webster rang me to say the developers were releasing the third phase of housing plots that day, so I had the plans couriered over to me at the Palace hotel. Rachael picked the plot that she liked, overlooking the 14th, 15th, 16th and 17th holes, but time was of the essence if we were to bag it. We told Graham which one we liked and he agreed to go and take pictures of the plot straight away. Unfortunately, the weather was wet and misty so when he emailed them to us at the hotel all we could see was what looked like a potato field, but he said it was a superb site and so I bought the plot, unseen. It was something I would definitely not have done a few years before.

Here I was, fighting cancer, still not knowing if I was going to live or die, spending around £140,000 on a bit of land, next to a newly seeded golf course in the middle of nowhere, in a foreign country. Perhaps it made me more gung-ho, but I thought building a house in the sunshine would be therapeutic and a beautiful retreat in years to come. I have never regretted it, and we spend as many English winter months there as my cricket commentary work allows, and I love it.

When we returned from Sun City, the first thing I needed to do was go and see Catherine Coyle for my monthly check-up, and I handed back the feeding machine that had kept me alive for all those weeks. It was a momentous feeling as I looked at it and thought: 'I don't need you anymore, thank you very much.' Rachael's photo had done the trick, I was making myself eat and the fights between us had stopped.

Catherine had explained that while I was in remission for now, I would not be given the all-clear for five years. With my type of tongue cancer if it is going to come back, it does so in 80 per cent of cases within the first two years, so I would need a monthly check-up for the first year and then every two months in the second year. If it hadn't come back by then, there was still a 20 per cent chance, meaning my check-ups would be every three months in year three, every four months in year four and just two six months apart in year five.

She had already told me I was too weak to work that summer and said that my commentary career would need to be put on hold for some time, but I had to ease myself back into life in other ways. So I started accepting invitations to public events, something I had not normally done. If people were shocked when they saw me and how I looked, they were generally very kind and did not show it.

Rachael is also a good cook and loves entertaining, so for the first time in my life, having all this spare time on my hands meant we could start inviting friends over for lunch on a regular basis. On 26 April we had Fred Trueman and his wife Veronica, Richard and Allison Knaggs along with Martin Edwards and his then wife Sue.

Martin is a huge cricket fan and idolised Fred, but had never met him. You always worried with Fred whether he would take the story-telling too far, as he could show off in front of new people, but this day he was absolutely brilliant. He turned up in his big Rolls-Royce and had his dog with him, which he tied to a pear tree in our back garden. Throughout lunch he regaled us with stories for three hours about Len Hutton captaining in the West Indies, tales of Denis Compton, how quick Frank Tyson could bowl, and the day he met Harold Larwood.

He told Martin about meeting the 'three Ws' – Frank Worrell, Clyde Walcott and Everton Weekes – and how he had bowled to the great George Headley in his final Test on the 1953 tour to the West Indies. It was an outstanding performance from Fred, and he interspersed the cricketing tales with funny everyday jokes, but he never swore once and the girls were mesmerised by him. The funniest moment was when he just threw in the comment: 'And there's Len out on the balcony, giving this black girl one.' Martin's face was a picture when he replied to Fred: 'What! Sir Leonard?' He looked as if his boyhood dreams had just been shattered.

I was still exceptionally weak so in order to improve my fitness, I started Pilates classes most days at a gym in Wakefield. Rachael still needed to drive me, so said she would join in and keep an eye on me. Now she has always hated doing any exercise, but her idea was that she would get a flat stomach from the Pilates and I would get some muscles back. The instructor would give us exercises and stretching to do every day. It was as much as I could handle, because my muscles and ligaments had not been used for six months. It was funny though after a couple of weeks, when I got the flat stomach and Rachael the muscles, she decreed me well enough to drive myself and quit. I, on the other hand, really enjoyed it and my overall strength began to improve. My star nurse would still pop in to check up on me, and on 7 May we invited for tea the two ladies from the register office, Christine Smith and Norma Stroud, as a thank you for their help.

Later that month, I accepted an invitation for Rachael and me to be guests of the MCC at Lord's to watch a day of the Test match between England and Zimbabwe. This was my first cricket engagement since the cancer had been diagnosed. I was now back on familiar ground and if anyone asked about the cancer, I was honest but did not go into too much detail. It was a lovely time reconnecting with old friends but I got tired very quickly. The talking and travelling drained me and I soon wanted to go home.

The monthly check-ups were mentally exhausting. In the week or so leading up to each one, I would be nervous, then after I'd had the results I could relax for a couple of weeks before the nerves would start all over again. I knew if the cancer came back, it would be very hard to beat for a second time. This dread of Catherine Coyle finding something at each clinic was always there. I was not fearful exactly, but I knew I was under the cosh. Just because you have gone through months of gruelling treatment and the medical profession has done its best, it does not guarantee you will live.

To give myself the best chance, I was continuing with the new diet and vitamin supplements. The feng shui master visited us again on Friday 30 May to check the house and ensure everything was aligned properly. I needed as much reassurance as I could get and was always searching for diversions. As Rachael said, in reality I was bored so she got out hundreds of black and white pictures of my playing career and suggested I write on the back the date, venue and name of anyone else on the picture and then file them away in order of the year. She joked that way they would be worth more when I was dead.

A few weeks later, on 19 June, I was asked to appear on *This Is Your Life* for Alec Stewart. I liked Alec and had great respect for him. I always admired his professionalism and the fastidious care he took over his appearance. He should have got more recognition for his wicketkeeping, as he missed very little, and he was also a bloody good batsman on the front or back foot. To be honest I didn't really want to go all that way down to London for the show, but for him I made the effort. None of my suits fitted me and were all hanging off my skinny frame, but we managed to find one that was just about presentable. Even though they put me on last, it was still very exhausting and a reminder for me not to run before I could walk, but I was glad we went.

Towards the end of the month who should come for lunch but my great friend Brian Clough and his wife Barbara. He'd decided to come see for himself how I was. Brian was in good form, always interesting and made me laugh.

Throughout this period I had received many press requests for interviews. The late Lynda Lee Potter, of the *Daily Mail*, was one journalist who kept in constant touch, particularly with Rachael. I agreed she could actually come to my home to have an exclusive interview. I did not request any money. Lynda was charming but it was dangerous to underestimate her; she always gave me the impression that she was like that delightful Miss Marple from St Mary Mead. Lynda had a sharp brain taking everything in and quickly worked out the secret of my strength and always used to write: 'The great cricketer is lucky to have married Rachael.' Well as you can imagine, Rachael loved that. I still tease her even now, that she is lucky I married her.

By July I had started to write copy myself for my column in the *Daily Telegraph*. Rachael and I got our first invite to Fred's house for lunch, along with Brian Close, his wife Vivian and Ray Illingworth and wife Shirley. Now who would have believed that a few years earlier, during all the troubles between us. I had never been to the Truemans' house and found they had this gorgeous cottage with a beautiful garden overlooking the Yorkshire Dales. Fred was keen on birdlife and used to sit watching the birds from his lounge. There was a lot more to Fred Trueman than people think.

For some time, Mark Nicholas had been pressing me to give an interview on Channel 4 television about my recovery, but I was reluctant to do it as I did not want to tempt fate. I still had a long way to go and didn't know if I was going to live or die. People also get confused between 'in remission' and 'being cured', and I was still only in the first stage. However, feeling physically and mentally stronger in myself, I agreed to do a live interview with Mark during the Leeds Test match. I also gave one to Sky TV and to Jonathan Agnew on BBC's *Test Match Special*.

I did not realise it at the time, but this was the start of my getting on with my working life again. In September, I was asked by ESPN to fly to India for some promotional work, and when Catherine Coyle said it would be okay to go, I was happy to repay them for their continued support. I started in Delhi and had a three-hour session with the Indian media, which was like a rugby scrum. There were ten times more cameras than you would see at a press conference in England. I was also taken to visit a cancer hospital, then did shows with Sunil Gavaskar in Delhi and Calcutta. I ended up going to Singapore, where Rachael and Emma joined me, and did a programme in the ESPN studio talking about Sachin Tendulkar. It was a public relations exercise which I was thrilled to do and be a part of. I loved it all, finally arriving home on 31 October.

The next few weeks saw me gradually increase my workload almost back up to normal levels. I attended the opening of the ECB's Cricket Academy at Loughborough University and even had to stand in for the Queen, who was running late and helped fill in the time before her arrival by doing a question and answer session with Jonathan Agnew.

Two days later, we went over to Thorp Arch, near Wetherby, to the training ground of Leeds United Football Club. Jonny Bairstow was playing for Leeds Under-15s and I went to see how he played. Rachael had become very close to his mother Janet, after her husband David's death in January 1998 and we had looked out for her and closely watched young Jonny and his sister Becky grow up ever since. Janet was concerned that Jonathan was doing too much: he was playing rugby for Yorkshire schools, training for Yorkshire cricket's academy side and playing football for Leeds United. She asked me to have a word with him, but before that I needed to satisfy myself how he performed in all these sports. I told him he needed to give up one winter sport, in order to do justice to the other two. Which sport? He must decide which he liked the least, and football was the answer.

I left for Australia on 29 November for my first commentary gig since the cancer diagnosis. ESPN were covering the

Australia–India series and they promised me I could come off air at any time if I felt tired; it was a wonderful trip and I felt alive again. I was careful to avoid anyone with a runny nose, or a cold. My immune system took another two years to recover, so I was very wary of catching a virus and kept up the old Vaseline trick as a matter of course every morning.

Rachael and Emma came over for the Christmas holidays and we attended the famous Carols by Candlelight service in Melbourne on Christmas Eve, which Tony Greig had organised tickets for. This sort of thing would never have interested me before, but it was quite magical being able to watch the wonder and delight on my daughter's face. For New Year, we stayed at the Park Hyatt hotel in Sydney, overlooking Circular Quay and had a great view for the New Year's Eve fireworks, another poignant moment because I had not been sure I would make it so far as to see in another new year.

Catherine Coyle had agreed to my trip only if I agreed to see another oncologist for my check-ups, so I arranged to visit a Dr Patrick Bridger in Bankstown, Sydney. He had a look down my throat and reported all looked well and I could carry on with the rest of the tour, finally arriving home on 10 February. It was a long trip but I got through it with a bit of common sense and help from ESPN.

Over the next four years, I went to see Catherine for my check-ups and she would poke her fingers down my throat. It never got any easier. Sitting there waiting for the verdict is like waiting for the umpire to put up his finger or say not out. I was lucky that she always said not out, which was an enormous relief.

For my last two visits, after Cookridge had closed down, I had to report to St James Hospital in Leeds. On my penultimate visit, Catherine was looking down my throat and poking around and said: 'Right! I will see you in six months and that will be your last check-up.' I was just going out the door and she said: 'By the way, it is getting close now you know.' And with that, she tapped her bottom. I had promised her at the start of my treatment, I would kiss her arse if she saved me and she hadn't forgotten. She said the nurses would be ready with their cameras. She not only helped save my life, but she did it with humour and I liked her and will always be grateful.

As Mr Li, the feng shui master, predicted, I went on to celebrate my 70th birthday and invited 70 guests. Catherine Coyle was first on the list, but unfortunately was away attending an important conference. After her name came Pat Bradley, the surgeon from Nottinghamshire and his wife, and also guardian angel nurse Julie Maltman, who in fact with her husband had become a regular guest at our home parties and they all came to help me celebrate.

I am always asked if cancer changed me. I don't think anybody can totally change what they are and the characteristics of their DNA and personality. I'd always been a strident individual, forthright and frank, and you can't totally change that, but I think cancer does smooth off a lot of the edges.

Feng shui also believes you are born with characteristics common to that year. Funnily enough Rachael, Emma and I were all born in a dragon year. The only difference is I am a 'metal' dragon, which means I am strong and determined; Emma is an 'earth' dragon and has a mind 'like a platinum bear trap' and is if anything even more strong-minded than me, but also has some of her mum's way with people. Fortunately for both of us, Rachael was born a 'water' dragon, which means like water, she will always find a way through and solve any problem. But if she gets really cross, which happens about five times a year, Emma and I both know to run.

Surviving cancer doesn't stop you getting angry or mad sometimes, but Rachael gave me the best advice which pops into my mind today whenever I lose my temper. She just said: 'Say to yourself: does it really matter?' That is the most important thing. Does it matter if someone cuts across in front of me in their car, or my hotel room is not ready or there is a confused telephone receptionist when I ring up to speak to someone? OK, I still feel anger but it subsides quicker now.

I have been lucky to have spent an extra 12 years of life with my wife and daughter and would rather like at least another 12, but if I die tomorrow I have had the pride of seeing that 14-year-old girl grow up into a beautiful young woman, qualify as a litigation lawyer and start her own Wedding and Events consultancy business. The medical profession are saving a lot of people and performing wonders, but unfortunately more people are contracting this disease and it is like trying to hold back the tide: you can only do so much, as it keeps on coming.

A cure doesn't seem any nearer, and as a cancer survivor you can never declare you have beaten it, or as we say in Yorkshire, licked it. It could come back any time. I am one of the lucky ones. I have been given a few extra years and I have learned to enjoy every single minute of life. Don't waste it, because you don't know how long you have got on this earth. It may be a lot less than three score and ten years.

I know some people will laugh and be sceptical, but I truly believe that following all the different routes I did, and continuing with some even today, helped to save me from cancer. I will never know why I am still alive. Was it Catherine Coyle and her NHS treatment? Was it the feng shui or Chris Woollams and Patrick Kingsley's knowledge and complementary medicine? Was it fate or was it a combination of all those things? Who knows? The only thing I really do know for certain is I would not have survived without my wife Rachael being there for me.

CHAPTER 6

EXPLODING THE PACKER MYTH

Cancer afflicts one in three people, and many of my friends have fought their own battles. Tony Greig was one of them, and he was diagnosed with lung cancer just two months before he died in Sydney of a heart attack at the age of 66 in December 2012.

Six months later, I went to his UK memorial service at St Martin-in-the-Fields Church in Trafalgar Square. It was a wonderful setting, with eulogies delivered by Richie Benaud, Dennis Amiss, Michael Holding and David Gower. The whole occasion was organised by the England and Wales Cricket Board in accordance with his widow Vivian's instructions, a final sign that Tony had been accepted by the English cricketing establishment he had battled for so long.

Benaud and Amiss spoke warmly of Tony the man, but of

course World Series Cricket and his ties to Kerry Packer were never far away. More than 30 years had passed since that terribly divisive time, and a new gloss put on the civil war, sparked by Packer and Greig, that gripped cricket between 1976 and 1978.

The memorial service was a chance to reflect on Tony's life in a celebratory, happy way. But unfortunately there was an awful lot of twaddle written and spoken about the Packer issue, and I left the service feeling angry that history had been rewritten by people who were not involved in the events at the time. The eulogies made Tony out to be a saint who saved cricketers from poverty and the clutches of over-bearing, controlling administrators.

It started when I picked up the order of service. There was a piece by Mike Atherton, reproduced from his column in *The Times*, which trotted out the same old guff about how Packer improved the lives of modern-day players. I like Mike's writing, but on this occasion he never told us how or gave us any specifics. He wrote: 'Every cricketer who has made even a half-decent living from the game since then owes Greig and his contemporaries a debt of gratitude for the battle won against the rapacious administrators of three decades ago.'

Rubbish! How could he know? He has no first-hand knowledge, as he was nine years old at the time of Packer. He fell into the same trap as a lot of people by thinking Greig and Packer were the saviours of our game, but I don't see it that way.

Tony's widow, Vivian, gave a long-winded lecture which made me want to stand up and leave. She hardly mentioned anything at all about Tony the man, the guy she married and what fun company he could be. Instead she appeared to want to settle a score in London against the British Establishment over Packer and World Series Cricket. She made him out to be an altruistic man who gave up the captaincy of England to benefit cricketers everywhere and suggested that we were all indebted to him. I sat there thinking: 'No, this is not right.' I found it sick-making. It was very far from my own experience of those times.

I wondered what Vivian could possibly know about those events. She was 17 at the time, so she can know only what Tony or the other World Series cricketers have told her. Over the years, she spent many hours at my house and I at hers and Packer cricket was never raised once by any of us. She, like Mike Atherton, had no personal knowledge of it, so they can't possibly comprehend the emotion and bitterness involved. They can have no idea of the resentment I felt sat there in the church about their version of events. At the time, you were either for or against Packer cricket; people became very entrenched in their views and it was a very unpleasant two-year period for the game, and we shouldn't pretend otherwise.

Packer touched upon issues of nationality and loyalty, for the players who signed up, and in particular for Tony Greig, and for those who didn't. The result was that it set friend against friend, as happened with Tony and me, and that is why it remains such a powerful issue to this day.

At the heart of the matter was a domineering giant of a man in Packer. Greigy, a flamboyant character who shared his new boss's ruthless ability to pursue his own agenda, was also a key figure in the story. It ended up in a High Court case and many of the people involved do not look back on it fondly. As each side tried to get its view heard, I ended up spending hours being cross-examined in the witness box, was rubbished in the press by Tony, and accused of pulling out of Packer cricket in a sulk over not being offered the captaincy. I was smeared and it hurt, but it was all rubbish. Tony, Kerry Packer and those who worked for him did a fantastic PR job making people believe their actions would change cricketers' lives for the better. But it wasn't like that.

I believe the whole Packer circus can be traced back to a blank winter for England in 1975–76. Tony had been made England captain earlier that year and, with no winter tour, he got an opportunity out of the blue to go to Australia to play for Waverley Cricket Club, near Bondi Beach in Sydney. He was not paid any money to play cricket, but the club said it would find him work and he would turn out for them as an amateur.

It was not hard to find him employment as Tony was not only a celebrity in 1970s Sydney, he had a huge personality and presence. He was made for television and this was spotted by one of the Waverley members, a man named Ian Macfarlane, who worked in advertising. He soon fixed him up with television contracts, a newspaper column and lots of commercial work. Tony loved it. He was perfect for it and he played absolutely fabulously for Waverley on Saturdays. He gained respect for his performances and made many friends. It laid the groundwork for what was to follow in 1977.

Before England left for India in late 1976, Tony had a couple of free months after the end of the season, which allowed him to have another quick trip to Sydney to do more television work and personal appearances. He did not play for Waverley this time and made the trip for purely commercial reasons. It was financially rewarding and a tremendous fillip for his ego.

You have to remember that in England in the 1970s, it was very difficult for sportsmen to find work in television advertising, or product endorsement. Actors and actresses took almost all the available spots. The actors' union, Equity, looked after its people very well and it was hard for cricketers, or any other sportsmen, to get a look-in. However, in Australia they did not have as many showbiz stars, so sportsmen were in greater demand, and Tony was able to cash in. If you were good, they idolised you and gave you opportunities. Sydney also offered sea, sunshine and a beautiful city, just what he had grown up with in South Africa. He felt very comfortable there and it gave him ideas for the future.

While he was on this trip, he recommended me to Waverley Cricket Club, as I wasn't playing for England at the time through my own choice. During this period, I spent quite a bit of time with Tony and his first wife Donna, and I would join them at their house where she would frequently cook for us both. I had first-hand knowledge of what he was thinking, and believe that this adventure into the commercial world of television made a big impact on him and changed his outlook on life, leading to massive consequences for the rest of us.

In the winter of 1976–77, while I was playing for Waverley, having taken Greigy's place, the same man who helped Tony, Ian Macfarlane, sorted me out with media work. I had two newspaper columns, with the *Sydney Daily Telegraph* and the *Sydney Morning Herald*, and TV commentary work with the 0-10 Network commentating on Sheffield Shield cricket.

I would have nets at Waverley on the Thursday then fly to

somewhere like Brisbane or Melbourne to commentate on the state game on the Friday. I would return to Sydney on Friday night and play for Waverley the following day. After I'd played, I would fly back to commentate on the end of the Shield game. The club also gave me a lovely battered old second-hand car and I had a fantastic time.

In January 1977 John Spencer of Sussex, who was coaching in Sydney, told me Kerry Packer would like me to go and look at his son. Kerry had a net in his back garden and I went to see young James bat. He was about nine years old and was a nice little batsman, but Kerry would not stop interrupting. The kid was nervous and always looking at his dad for approval while I was coaching him. Kerry was too overbearing and that is not good for kids, as it makes them concentrate more on pleasing Dad than on learning batting. I made him turn his back on his father, talk to me and listen to my advice not his dad's. Then his father said: 'I don't want him to be a professional cricketer because they don't earn anything.' It made me wonder why he'd asked me to go there.

I thought that would be the end with Kerry Packer, but soon after John Spencer said that Packer wanted to see me again, and this time it was about a coaching job for the following season. As I was a free agent in the winter months, I went to his offices in Sydney on Tuesday 8 March, just before the Centenary Test in Melbourne, and he said if I returned to Australia the following year he could give me a job coaching cricket in the territories outside the big cities of Australia. He asked what I would want financially and when I told him £20,000 to take on the role, he refused to pay that, so I got up to walk out. As I was about to leave, he said: 'Just a minute.

I have something else I want to talk to you about, but I need your assurance that whatever happens you will keep it confidential.'

He said he was going to put together some cricket matches in the next Australian season between a World XI and an Australian XI, which would include some of the players who had just retired such as Ian Chappell, Ross Edwards and Ian Redpath. Australia were due to play India that season, and he felt it would not be of much interest to the Australian public. He asked if I would be interested in playing for his World XI? I said yes, as I was hoping to come back anyway and play for Waverley in the English winter.

I had no idea he was setting himself up to go against established cricket, and I had no knowledge of his meeting with the Australian Cricket Board nine months earlier in June 1976, when he was refused the opportunity to bid for the Australian television cricket rights. How could I know this was the start of his scheming and plotting to get top-class cricket on his television station Channel 9? I also did not know this was a man not used to being turned down or not getting his own way. Only later did I realise all this, and that to Kerry money equalled power.

I thought he was going to sign players for exhibition matches, like the Rothmans International Cavaliers, who had played 40 overs per side on Sundays during the English summer. I had played for them a few times, and their sides tended to consist of current English players plus some already retired big-name players such as Denis Compton, Ted Dexter and Godfrey Evans. These matches were shown on BBC TV and big crowds came along.

Early days, preparing for the start of the 1965 season, having made my international debut the previous summer.

My last innings. Going out to bat with Ashley Metcalfe at Scarborough on 10 September 1986 in my final game.

David Lloyd and I survey the pitch at Bramall Lane, Sheffield, on 4 August 1973 – the last first-class match to be played there. *(Getty Images)*

With two great friends, Dickie Bird and Michael Parkinson at Lord's in 2005, celebrating Michael's 70th birthday.

I was very proud to accept the role as Yorkshire president, but sadly there were some who tried to stir up trouble before I took on the job.

Bob Appleyard, me, Raymond Illingworth and Phil Sharpe during my time as president of Yorkshire CCC.

Brian Clough takes over at Leeds United, and I joined him soon after this picture was taken. How I wish he'd been my cricket coach, rather than the greatest manager English football has ever produced. *(Mirrorpix)*

Manchester United are my favourite team, ever since Denis Law signed for them in 1962. Here I am with Sir Bobby Charlton and Martin Edwards, president of the club.

On holiday in the Caribbean with Richard Knaggs and Tony Greig in 2004. Sadly, so much twaddle has been spoken about the Packer affair, in which Tony played such a central role.

It was at the Lamb Inn in Rainton where I met Rachael, the love of my life.

Our wedding day on 26 February 2003. Because of my battle with cancer, I had lost so much weight that my suit almost drowned me.

Our house near Paarl in South Africa, overlooking a Jack Nicklaus-designed golf course. I bought the plot of land when I was battling against cancer.

Like peas in a pod: me and my daughter Emma as babies.

Emma changed my life in so many ways, as I had to adapt to new responsibilities. Here she is encouraging me to try out a swimming pool. Strange as it may seem, I'd always avoided them in the past.

Dancing with Emma on my 70th birthday.

The Indian cricket team came to visit me in my house in Woolley just after I had discovered a lump in my neck.

LEFT: With my brother Tony, who helped me so much during my illness.

BELOW LEFT: When I saw this picture, and how thin I had become during my battle with cancer, I knew I had to do something to regain my strength.

BELOW RIGHT: The mask I had to put on when I was having my chemotherapy.
(*Philip Brown*)

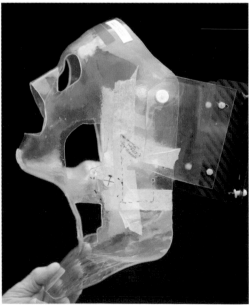

The curse of sledging is bringing down cricket. Here Michael Clarke confronts Jimmy Anderson during the Brisbane Test in November 2013. There was no excuse for what he said. *(Getty Images)*

It is crucial that Test cricket remains the pinnacle of the game – if it means adopting day/night matches with a pink ball to help draw in the crowds, I'm all for it. *(Getty Images)*

Kevin Pietersen tries to hit the ball for six during the Perth Test in December 2013, only to be caught on the boundary – it looked as if he did not give a damn. *(Getty Images)*

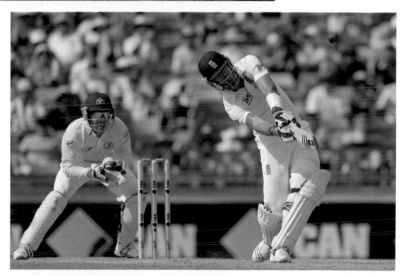

If England are to stand a chance in the Ashes series of 2015, they will have to learn how to handle the express pace of Mitchell Johnson. *(Getty Images)*

The new generation, with Joe Root among them, will play a vital role in next year's Ashes series. *(Getty Images)*